A Greek Prose Reading Course
for Post-Beginners

Unit 3. Political Oratory
Demosthenes: *Third Philippic*

With Commentary and
Vocabulary by
MALCOLM CAMPBELL

Bristol Classical Press

This impression 2004
First published in 1997 by
Bristol Classical Press
an imprint of
Gerald Duckworth & Co. Ltd.
90-93 Cowcross Street
London EC1M 6BF
Tel: 020 7490 7300
Fax: 020 7490 0080
inquiries@duckworth-publishers.co.uk
www.ducknet.co.uk

A catalogue record for this book is available
from the British Library

ISBN 1 85399 539 8

Printed and bound in Great Britain by
Antony Rowe Ltd, Eastbourne

UNIT 3. POLITICAL ORATORY

CONTENTS

PREFACE

My thanks to John Betts for giving this project a warm reception and for very helpful advice, and to his team at Bristol Classical Press, Jean Scott, Editor, and Graham Douglas in Production, for welcome assistance with typesetting; to my colleagues Professor Stephen Halliwell and Dr Niall Livingstone for taking the time to read the typescripts and for suggesting a number of improvements; to my wife Dorothy for her encouragement, patience and technical help; to my younger son Richard for devoting more than one long evening to explaining to me what I was unable to work out for myself through reading *Macs for Dummies*.

No two teachers of Greek are likely to agree for long on how textbooks of this nature should be formatted, let alone what sort of information, and how much information, they should contain. I have been guided here first and foremost by our own students at St Andrews: I am grateful to them for discussing their difficulties and needs with me, for filling in questionnaires, and for producing some useful feedback on the form and content of earlier drafts of the Lysias and Plato texts. I must thank too a class of Bristol undergraduates whom I have never met, for offering general comment on the Lysias notes circulated to them in 1996 through the kind offices of John Betts and Onno van Nijf.

St Andrews, February 1997   M.C.

GENERAL INTRODUCTION TO THE COURSE

Represented in this course are three of the giants among prose writers of the Classical period, the historian Thucydides, the philosopher Plato, the orator Demosthenes. The same ancient literary critic (Dionysius of Halicarnassus) who called Demosthenes' *Philippic* iii "the greatest of the public orations directed against Philip" also found much to admire in the speeches of Lysias (see M. Edwards and S. Usher, *Greek Orators* I [Warminster, 1985], 128-9). There is certainly much to interest the modern reader in *On the Murder of Eratosthenes.*

In annotating these texts I have tried to keep the needs of three classes of reader constantly in mind:
Students fresh from Beginners courses (whether at University or elsewhere) reading an extended (and undoctored) Greek text for the first time.
Post-A-level (or equivalent) students who wish to consolidate their reading skills.
Postgraduate students who have some Greek but require guidance in reading an historical, oratorical or philosophical text in the original.

Since each unit is self-contained, those with an interest in Socrates, for example, can take on *Crito* right away. But post-Beginners are advised to read the Lysias speech before anything else: it is an excellent starter-text, and for that reason extra help has been given with the verbal systems. For the benefit of those who do choose to take on the course in its entirety the other three components have been given different emphases: in the Plato special attention is paid to the use of particles and particle-combinations, in the Demosthenes (a prime model for the few who still do Greek prose composition) to a number of key differences between Greek and English idiom; the Thucydides approximates more closely to the kind of commentary students will encounter if they carry their Greek studies further, with more extensive coverage of the subject-matter and explicit references to secondary literature. One possible programme, extending over two or three semesters: Lysias, Plato, Demosthenes and/ or Thucydides interspersed with a play of Euripides or Sophocles and a book or two of Homer.

For all four units the layout is essentially the same, and recommendations on study-methods are given in the respective prefaces:
1 Greek text. Observations are made from time to time in the Notes on the constitution of the text, and those who wish to pursue these matters further may consult the following editions, in which a critical apparatus (*apparatus criticus*) is

printed at the bottom of the page, where the editor, communicating in Latin, records variant readings in ancient and mediaeval copies (identified in the "Sigla" prefacing the text itself) and points to places where modern scholars have felt dissatisfied with the transmitted text and considered it necessary to emend:

Lysias, Oxford text by K. Hude (1912), see also the edition by C. Carey (1989), pp.12-13

Plato, Oxford text by E.A. Duke and others (1995)

Demosthenes, Oxford text by S.H. Butcher (1903), Budé text by M. Croiset (1955)

Thucydides, Budé text by J. de Romilly (1967), Oxford text by H.S. Jones and J.E. Powell (2nd edn, 1942).

2 Preliminary remarks on word formation and syntax geared to the text in question. Common to all: a systematic analysis of Perfects/ Pluperfects (usually viewed with dread by post-Beginners, in my experience), and a review of the uses of Subjunctive and Optative.

3 A brief outline of the entire work/ extract.

4 A summary of the content of each block of text.

5 Dedicated vocabularies, broken down into the various parts of speech. The words within each category are arranged alphabetically according to type: in the case of verbs, for example, infinitives in -ειν -εσθαι, then contracted forms -ᾶν -ᾶσθαι/ -εῖν -εῖσθαι/ -οῦν -οῦσθαι, and finally -ναι -σθαι.

6 Notes dealing with language, style and subject-matter.

7 It is envisaged that the material on each of the texts provided here will be topped up by tutors with a course of lectures dealing with author, genre, general background, broad issues and particular problems of interpretation. Those going it alone will find something to suit most tastes in the secondary literature specified in the suggestions for further reading.

ΔΗΜΟΣΘΕΝΟΥΣ
ΚΑΤΑ ΦΙΛΙΠΠΟΥ Γ

1 Πολλῶν, ὦ ἄνδρες Ἀθηναῖοι, λόγων γιγνομένων ὀλίγου δεῖν καθ' ἑκάστην ἐκκλησίαν περὶ ὧν Φίλιππος, ἀφ' οὗ τὴν εἰρήνην ἐποιήσατο, οὐ μόνον ὑμᾶς, ἀλλὰ καὶ τοὺς ἄλλους ἀδικεῖ, καὶ πάντων οἶδ' ὅτι φησάντων γ' ἄν, εἰ καὶ μὴ ποιοῦσι τοῦτο, καὶ λέγειν δεῖν καὶ πράττειν ὅπως ἐκεῖνος παύσεται τῆς ὕβρεως καὶ δίκην δώσει, εἰς τοῦθ' ὑπηγμένα πάντα τὰ πράγματα καὶ προειμέν' ὁρῶ, ὥστε δέδοικα μὴ βλάσφημον μὲν εἰπεῖν, ἀληθὲς δ' ᾖ· εἰ καὶ λέγειν ἅπαντες ἐβούλονθ' οἱ παριόντες καὶ χειροτονεῖν ὑμεῖς ἐξ ὧν ὡς φαυλότατ' ἔμελλε τὰ πράγμαθ' ἕξειν, οὐκ ἂν ἡγοῦμαι δύνασθαι χεῖρον ἢ νῦν διατεθῆναι. 2 πολλὰ μὲν οὖν ἴσως ἐστὶν αἴτια τούτων, καὶ οὐ παρ' ἓν οὐδὲ δύ' εἰς τοῦτο τὰ πράγματ' ἀφῖκται· μάλιστα δ', ἄνπερ ἐξετάζητ' ὀρθῶς, εὑρήσετε διὰ τοὺς χαρίζεσθαι μᾶλλον ἢ τὰ βέλτιστα λέγειν προαιρουμένους, ὧν τινες μέν, ὦ ἄνδρες Ἀθηναῖοι, ἐν οἷς εὐδοκιμοῦσιν αὐτοὶ καὶ δύνανται, ταῦτα φυλάττοντες οὐδεμίαν περὶ τῶν μελλόντων πρόνοιαν ἔχουσιν, {οὐκοῦν οὐδ' ὑμᾶς οἴονται δεῖν ἔχειν,} ἕτεροι δὲ τοὺς ἐπὶ τοῖς πράγμασιν ὄντας αἰτιώμενοι καὶ διαβάλλοντες οὐδὲν ἄλλο ποιοῦσιν ἢ ὅπως ἡ πόλις αὐτὴ παρ' αὑτῆς δίκην λήψεται καὶ περὶ τοῦτ' ἔσται, Φιλίππῳ δ' ἔξεσται καὶ λέγειν καὶ πράττειν ὅ τι βούλεται. 3 αἱ δὲ τοιαῦται πολιτεῖαι συνήθεις μέν εἰσιν ὑμῖν, αἴτιαι δὲ τῶν κακῶν. ἀξιῶ δ', ὦ ἄνδρες Ἀθηναῖοι, ἄν τι τῶν ἀληθῶν μετὰ παρρησίας λέγω, μηδεμίαν μοι διὰ τοῦτο παρ' ὑμῶν ὀργὴν γενέσθαι. σκοπεῖτε γὰρ ὡδί· ὑμεῖς τὴν παρρησίαν ἐπὶ μὲν τῶν ἄλλων οὕτω κοινὴν οἴεσθε δεῖν εἶναι πᾶσι τοῖς ἐν τῇ πόλει, ὥστε καὶ τοῖς ξένοις καὶ τοῖς δούλοις αὐτῆς μεταδεδώκατε, καὶ πολλοὺς ἄν τις οἰκέτας ἴδοι παρ' ἡμῖν μετὰ πλείονος ἐξουσίας ὅ τι βούλονται λέγοντας ἢ πολίτας ἐν ἐνίαις τῶν ἄλλων πόλεων, ἐκ δὲ τοῦ συμβουλεύειν παντάπασιν ἐξεληλάκατε. 4 εἶθ' ὑμῖν συμβέβηκεν ἐκ τούτου ἐν μὲν ταῖς ἐκκλησίαις τρυφᾶν καὶ κολακεύεσθαι πάντα πρὸς ἡδονὴν ἀκούουσιν, ἐν δὲ τοῖς πράγμασι καὶ τοῖς γιγνομένοις περὶ τῶν ἐσχάτων ἤδη κινδυνεύειν. εἰ μὲν οὖν καὶ νῦν οὕτω διάκεισθε, οὐκ ἔχω τί λέγω· εἰ δ' ἃ συμφέρει χωρὶς κολακείας ἐθελήσετ' ἀκούειν, ἕτοιμος λέγειν. καὶ γὰρ εἰ πάνυ φαύλως τὰ πράγματ' ἔχει καὶ πολλὰ προεῖται, ὅμως ἔστιν, ἐὰν ὑμεῖς τὰ δέοντα ποιεῖν βούλησθε, ἔτι πάντα ταῦτ' ἐπανορθώσασθαι. 5 καὶ παράδοξον μὲν ἴσως ἐστὶν ὃ μέλλω λέγειν, ἀληθὲς δέ· τὸ χείριστον ἐν τοῖς παρεληλυθόσι, τοῦτο πρὸς τὰ μέλλοντα βέλτιστον ὑπάρχει. τί οὖν ἐστι τοῦτο; ὅτι οὔτε μικρὸν οὔτε μέγ' οὐδὲν τῶν δεόντων ποιούντων ὑμῶν κακῶς τὰ πράγματ' ἔχει, ἐπεί τοι, εἰ πάνθ' ἃ προσῆκε πραττόντων οὕτως διέκειτο, οὐδ' ἂν ἐλπὶς ἦν αὐτὰ γενέσθαι βελτίω. νῦν δὲ τῆς ῥᾳθυμίας τῆς ὑμετέρας καὶ τῆς ἀμελείας κεκράτηκε Φίλιππος, τῆς πόλεως δ' οὐ κεκράτηκεν· οὐδ' ἥττησθ' ὑμεῖς, ἀλλ' οὐδὲ κεκίνησθε.

{6 Εἰ μὲν οὖν ἅπαντες ὡμολογοῦμεν Φίλιππον τῇ πόλει πολεμεῖν καὶ τὴν εἰρήνην παραβαίνειν, οὐδὲν ἄλλ᾽ ἔδει τὸν παριόντα λέγειν καὶ συμβουλεύειν ἢ ὅπως ἀσφαλέστατα καὶ ῥᾷστ᾽ αὐτὸν ἀμυνούμεθα· ἐπειδὴ δ᾽ οὕτως ἀτόπως ἔνιοι διάκεινται, ὥστε πόλεις καταλαμβάνοντος ἐκείνου καὶ πολλὰ τῶν ὑμετέρων ἔχοντος καὶ πάντας ἀνθρώπους ἀδικοῦντος ἀνέχεσθαί τινων ἐν ταῖς ἐκκλησίαις λεγόντων πολλάκις ὡς ἡμῶν τινές εἰσιν οἱ ποιοῦντες τὸν πόλεμον, ἀνάγκη φυλάττεσθαι καὶ διορθοῦσθαι περὶ τούτου. 7 ἔστι γὰρ δέος μήποθ᾽ ὡς ἀμυνούμεθα γράψας τις καὶ συμβουλεύσας εἰς τὴν αἰτίαν ἐμπέσῃ τοῦ πεποιηκέναι τὸν πόλεμον. ἐγὼ δὴ τοῦτο πρῶτον ἁπάντων λέγω καὶ διορίζομαι· εἰ ἐφ᾽ ἡμῖν ἐστι τὸ βουλεύεσθαι περὶ τοῦ πότερον εἰρήνην ἄγειν ἢ πολεμεῖν δεῖ ... } 8 εἰ μὲν οὖν ἔξεστιν εἰρήνην ἄγειν τῇ πόλει καὶ ἐφ᾽ ἡμῖν ἐστι τοῦτο, ἵν᾽ ἐντεῦθεν ἄρξωμαι, φήμ᾽ ἔγωγ᾽ ἄγειν ἡμᾶς δεῖν, καὶ τὸν ταῦτα λέγοντα γράφειν καὶ πράττειν καὶ μὴ φενακίζειν ἀξιῶ· εἰ δ᾽ ἕτερος τὰ ὅπλ᾽ ἐν ταῖς χερσὶν ἔχων καὶ δύναμιν πολλὴν περὶ αὐτὸν τοὔνομα μὲν τὸ τῆς εἰρήνης ὑμῖν προβάλλει, τοῖς δ᾽ ἔργοις αὐτὸς τοῖς τοῦ πολέμου χρῆται, τί λοιπὸν ἄλλο πλὴν ἀμύνεσθαι; φάσκειν δ᾽ εἰρήνην ἄγειν εἰ βούλεσθε, ὥσπερ ἐκεῖνος, οὐ διαφέρομαι. 9 εἰ δέ τις ταύτην εἰρήνην ὑπολαμβάνει, ἐξ ἧς ἐκεῖνος πάντα τἄλλα λαβὼν ἐφ᾽ ἡμᾶς ἥξει, πρῶτον μὲν μαίνεται, ἔπειτ᾽ ἐκείνῳ παρ᾽ ὑμῶν, οὐχ ὑμῖν παρ᾽ ἐκείνου τὴν εἰρήνην λέγει· τοῦτο δ᾽ ἐστὶν ὃ τῶν ἀναλισκομένων χρημάτων πάντων Φίλιππος ὠνεῖται, αὐτὸς μὲν πολεμεῖν ὑμῖν, ὑφ᾽ ὑμῶν δὲ μὴ πολεμεῖσθαι.

10 Καὶ μὴν εἰ μέχρι τούτου περιμενοῦμεν, ἕως ἂν ἡμῖν ὁμολογήσῃ πολεμεῖν, πάντων ἐσμὲν εὐηθέστατοι· οὐδὲ γὰρ ἂν ἐπὶ τὴν Ἀττικὴν αὐτὴν βαδίζῃ καὶ τὸν Πειραιᾶ, τοῦτ᾽ ἐρεῖ, εἴπερ οἷς πρὸς τοὺς ἄλλους πεποίηκε δεῖ τεκμαίρεσθαι. 11 τοῦτο μὲν γὰρ Ὀλυνθίοις, τετταράκοντ᾽ ἀπέχων τῆς πόλεως στάδια, εἶπεν ὅτι δεῖ δυοῖν θάτερον, ἢ ἐκείνους ἐν Ὀλύνθῳ μὴ οἰκεῖν ἢ αὐτὸν ἐν Μακεδονίᾳ, πάντα τὸν ἄλλον χρόνον, εἴ τις αὐτὸν αἰτιάσαιτό τι τοιοῦτον, ἀγανακτῶν καὶ πρέσβεις πέμπων τοὺς ἀπολογησομένους· τοῦτο δ᾽ εἰς Φωκέας ὡς πρὸς συμμάχους ἐπορεύετο, καὶ πρέσβεις Φωκέων ἦσαν οἳ παρηκολούθουν αὐτῷ πορευομένῳ, καὶ παρ᾽ ἡμῖν ἤριζον οἱ πολλοὶ Θηβαίοις οὐ λυσιτελήσειν τὴν ἐκείνου πάροδον. 12 καὶ μὴν καὶ Φερὰς πρώην ὡς φίλος καὶ σύμμαχος εἰς Θετταλίαν ἐλθὼν ἔχει καταλαβών, καὶ τὰ τελευταῖα τοῖς ταλαιπώροις Ὠρείταις τουτοισὶ ἐπισκεψομένους ἔφη τοὺς στρατιώτας πεπομφέναι κατ᾽ εὔνοιαν· πυνθάνεσθαι γὰρ αὐτοὺς ὡς νοσοῦσι καὶ στασιάζουσιν, συμμάχων δ᾽ εἶναι καὶ φίλων ἀληθινῶν ἐν τοῖς τοιούτοις καιροῖς παρεῖναι. 13 εἶτ᾽ οἴεσθ᾽ αὐτόν, οἳ ἐποίησαν μὲν οὐδὲν ἂν κακόν, μὴ παθεῖν δ᾽ ἐφυλάξαντ᾽ ἂν ἴσως, τούτους μὲν ἐξαπατᾶν αἱρεῖσθαι μᾶλλον ἢ προλέγοντα βιάζεσθαι, ὑμῖν δ᾽ ἐκ προρρήσεως πολεμήσειν, καὶ ταῦθ᾽ ἕως ἂν ἑκόντες ἐξαπατᾶσθε; 14 οὐκ ἔστι ταῦτα· καὶ γὰρ ἂν ἀβελτερώτατος εἴη πάντων ἀνθρώπων, εἰ τῶν ἀδικουμένων ὑμῶν μηδὲν ἐγκαλούντων αὐτῷ, ἀλλ᾽ ὑμῶν αὐτῶν τινας αἰτιωμένων, ἐκεῖνος ἐκλύσας τὴν πρὸς ἀλλήλους ἔριν ὑμῶν καὶ φιλονικίαν ἐφ᾽ αὑτὸν προείποι

2

τρέπεσθαι, καὶ τῶν παρ' ἑαυτοῦ μισθοφορούντων τοὺς λόγους ἀφέλοιτο, οἷς ἀναβάλλουσιν ὑμᾶς, λέγοντες ὡς ἐκεῖνός γ' οὐ πολεμεῖ τῇ πόλει.

15 Ἀλλ' ἔστιν, ὦ πρὸς τοῦ Διός, ὅστις εὖ φρονῶν ἐκ τῶν ὀνομάτων μᾶλλον ἢ τῶν πραγμάτων τὸν ἄγοντ' εἰρήνην ἢ πολεμοῦνθ' αὑτῷ σκέψαιτ' ἄν; οὐδεὶς δήπου. ὁ τοίνυν Φίλιππος ἐξ ἀρχῆς, ἄρτι τῆς εἰρήνης γεγονυίας, οὔπω Διοπείθους στρατηγοῦντος οὐδὲ τῶν ὄντων ἐν Χερρονήσῳ νῦν ἀπεσταλμένων, Σέρριον καὶ Δορίσκον ἐλάμβανε καὶ τοὺς ἐκ Σερρείου τείχους καὶ Ἱεροῦ ὄρους στρατιώτας ἐξέβαλλεν, οὓς ὁ ὑμέτερος στρατηγὸς κατέστησεν. 16 καίτοι ταῦτα πράττων τί ἐποίει; εἰρήνην μὲν γὰρ ὠμωμόκει. καὶ μηδεὶς εἴπῃ, "τί δὲ ταῦτ' ἐστίν;" ἢ "τί τούτων μέλει τῇ πόλει;" εἰ μὲν γὰρ μικρὰ ταῦτα, ἢ μηδὲν ὑμῖν αὐτῶν ἔμελεν, ἄλλος ἂν εἴη λόγος οὗτος· τὸ δ' εὐσεβὲς καὶ τὸ δίκαιον, ἄν τ' ἐπὶ μικροῦ τις ἄν τ' ἐπὶ μείζονος παραβαίνῃ, τὴν αὐτὴν ἔχει δύναμιν. φέρε δή νῦν, ἡνίκ' εἰς Χερρόνησον, ἣν βασιλεὺς καὶ πάντες οἱ Ἕλληνες ὑμετέραν ἐγνώκασιν εἶναι, ξένους εἰσπέμπει καὶ βοηθεῖν ὁμολογεῖ καὶ ἐπιστέλλει ταῦτα, τί ποιεῖ; 17 φησὶ μὲν γὰρ οὐ πολεμεῖν, ἐγὼ δὲ τοσούτου δέω ταῦτα ποιοῦντ' ἐκεῖνον ἄγειν ὁμολογεῖν τὴν πρὸς ὑμᾶς εἰρήνην, ὥστε καὶ Μεγάρων ἁπτόμενον κἀν Εὐβοίᾳ τυραννίδα κατασκευάζοντα καὶ νῦν ἐπὶ Θρᾴκην παριόντα καὶ τἀν Πελοποννήσῳ σκευωρούμενον καὶ πάνθ' ὅσα πράττει μετὰ τῆς δυνάμεως ποιοῦντα, λύειν φημὶ τὴν εἰρήνην καὶ πολεμεῖν ὑμῖν, εἰ μὴ καὶ τοὺς τὰ μηχανήματ' ἐφιστάντας εἰρήνην ἄγειν φήσετε, ἕως ἂν αὐτὰ τοῖς τείχεσιν ἤδη προσαγάγωσιν. ἀλλ' οὐ φήσετε· ὁ γὰρ οἷς ἂν ἐγὼ ληφθείην, ταῦτα πράττων καὶ κατασκευαζόμενος, οὗτος ἐμοὶ πολεμεῖ, κἂν μήπω βάλλῃ μηδὲ τοξεύῃ. 18 τίσιν οὖν ὑμεῖς κινδυνεύσαιτ' ἄν, εἴ τι γένοιτο; τῷ τὸν Ἑλλήσποντον ἀλλοτριωθῆναι, τῷ Μεγάρων καὶ τῆς Εὐβοίας τὸν πολεμοῦνθ' ὑμῖν γενέσθαι κύριον, τῷ Πελοποννησίους τἀκείνου φρονῆσαι. εἶτα τὸν τοῦτο τὸ μηχάνημ' ἐπὶ τὴν πόλιν ἱστάντα, τοῦτον εἰρήνειν ἄγειν ἐγὼ φῶ πρὸς ὑμᾶς; 19 πολλοῦ γε καὶ δεῖ, ἀλλ' ἀφ' ἧς ἡμέρας ἀνεῖλε Φωκέας, ἀπὸ ταύτης ἔγωγ' αὐτὸν πολεμεῖν ὁρίζομαι. ὑμᾶς δ', ἐὰν ἀμύνησθ' ἤδη, σωφρονήσειν φημί, ἐὰν δ' ἐάσητε, οὐδὲ τοῦθ' ὅταν βούλησθε δυνήσεσθαι ποιῆσαι. καὶ τοσοῦτόν γ' ἀφέστηκα τῶν ἄλλων, ὦ ἄνδρες Ἀθηναῖοι, τῶν συμβουλευόντων, ὥστ' οὐδὲ δοκεῖ μοι περὶ Χερρονήσου νῦν σκοπεῖν οὐδὲ Βυζαντίου, 20 ἀλλ' ἐπαμῦναι μὲν τούτοις, καὶ διατηρῆσαι μή τι πάθωσι, {καὶ τοῖς οὖσιν ἐκεῖ νῦν στρατιώταις πάνθ' ὅσων ἂν δέωνται ἀποστεῖλαι,} βουλεύεσθαι μέντοι περὶ πάντων τῶν Ἑλλήνων ὡς ἐν κινδύνῳ μεγάλῳ καθεστώτων. βούλομαι δ' εἰπεῖν πρὸς ὑμᾶς ἐξ ὧν ὑπὲρ τῶν πραγμάτων οὕτω φοβοῦμαι, ἵν', εἰ μὲν ὀρθῶς λογίζομαι, μετάσχητε τῶν λογισμῶν καὶ πρόνοιάν τιν' ὑμῶν γ' αὐτῶν, εἰ μὴ καὶ τῶν ἄλλων ἄρα βούλεσθε, ποιήσησθε, ἂν δὲ ληρεῖν καὶ τετυφῶσθαι δοκῶ, μήτε νῦν μήτ' αὖθις ὡς ὑγιαίνοντί μοι προσέχητε.

3

ΔΗΜΟΣΘΕΝΟΥΣ

21 Ὅτι μὲν δὴ μέγας ἐκ μικροῦ καὶ ταπεινοῦ τὸ κατ' ἀρχὰς Φίλιππος ηὔξηται, καὶ ἀπίστως καὶ στασιαστικῶς ἔχουσι πρὸς αὐτοὺς οἱ Ἕλληνες, καὶ ὅτι πολλῷ παραδοξότερον ἦν τοσοῦτον αὐτὸν ἐξ ἐκείνου γενέσθαι ἢ νῦν, ὅθ' οὕτω πολλὰ προείληφε, καὶ τὰ λοιπὰ ὑφ' αὑτῷ ποιήσασθαι, καὶ πάνθ' ὅσα τοιαῦτ' ἂν ἔχοιμι διεξελθεῖν, παραλείψω. **22** ἀλλ' ὁρῶ συγκεχωρηκότας ἅπαντας ἀνθρώπους, ἀφ' ὑμῶν ἀρξαμένους, αὐτῷ, ὑπὲρ οὗ τὸν ἄλλον ἅπαντα χρόνον πάντες οἱ πόλεμοι γεγόνασιν οἱ Ἑλληνικοί. τί οὖν ἐστι τοῦτο; τὸ ποιεῖν ὅ τι βούλεται, καὶ καθ' ἕν' οὑτωσὶ περικόπτειν καὶ λωποδυτεῖν τῶν Ἑλλήνων, καὶ καταδουλοῦσθαι τὰς πόλεις ἐπιόντα. **23** καίτοι προστάται μὲν ὑμεῖς ἑβδομήκοντ' ἔτη καὶ τρία τῶν Ἑλλήνων ἐγένεσθε, προστάται δὲ τριάκονθ' ἑνὸς δέοντα Λακεδαιμόνιοι· ἴσχυσαν δέ τι καὶ Θηβαῖοι τουτουσὶ τοὺς τελευταίους χρόνους μετὰ τὴν ἐν Λεύκτροις μάχην. ἀλλ' ὅμως οὔθ' ὑμῖν οὔτε Θηβαίοις οὔτε Λακεδαιμονίοις οὐδεπώποτ', ὦ ἄνδρες Ἀθηναῖοι, συνεχωρήθη τοῦθ' ὑπὸ τῶν Ἑλλήνων, ποιεῖν ὅ τι βούλοισθε, οὐδὲ πολλοῦ δεῖ, **24** ἀλλὰ τοῦτο μὲν ὑμῖν, μᾶλλον δὲ τοῖς τότ' οὖσιν Ἀθηναίοις, ἐπειδή τισιν οὐ μετρίως ἐδόκουν προσφέρεσθαι, πάντες ᾤοντο δεῖν, καὶ οἱ μηδὲν ἐγκαλεῖν ἔχοντες αὐτοῖς, μετὰ τῶν ἠδικημένων πολεμεῖν· καὶ πάλιν Λακεδαιμονίοις ἄρξασι καὶ παρελθοῦσιν εἰς τὴν αὐτὴν δυναστείαν ὑμῖν, ἐπειδὴ πλεονάζειν ἐπεχείρουν καὶ πέρα τοῦ μετρίου τὰ καθεστηκότ' ἐκίνουν, πάντες εἰς πόλεμον κατέστησαν, καὶ οἱ μηδὲν ἐγκαλοῦντες αὐτοῖς. **25** καὶ τί δεῖ τοὺς ἄλλους λέγειν; ἀλλ' ἡμεῖς αὐτοὶ καὶ Λακεδαιμόνιοι, οὐδὲν ἂν εἰπεῖν ἔχοντες ἐξ ἀρχῆς ὅ τι ἠδικούμεθ' ὑπ' ἀλλήλων, ὅμως ὑπὲρ ὧν τοὺς ἄλλους ἀδικουμένους ἑωρῶμεν, πολεμεῖν ᾠόμεθα δεῖν. καίτοι πάνθ' ὅσ' ἐξημάρτηται καὶ Λακεδαιμονίοις ἐν τοῖς τριάκοντ' ἐκείνοις ἔτεσιν καὶ τοῖς ἡμετέροις προγόνοις ἐν τοῖς ἑβδομήκοντα, ἐλάττον' ἐστίν, ὦ ἄνδρες Ἀθηναῖοι, ὧν Φίλιππος ἐν τρισὶ καὶ δέκ' οὐχ ὅλοις ἔτεσιν, οἷς ἐπιπολάζει, ἠδίκηκε τοὺς Ἕλληνας — μᾶλλον δ' οὐδὲ μέρος τούτων ἐκεῖνα. **26** {καὶ τοῦτ' ἐκ βραχέος λόγου ῥᾴδιον δεῖξαι.} Ὄλυνθον μὲν δὴ καὶ Μεθώνην καὶ Ἀπολλωνίαν καὶ δύο καὶ τριάκοντα πόλεις ἐπὶ Θρᾴκης ἐῶ, ἃς ἁπάσας οὕτως ὠμῶς ἀνῄρηκεν ὥστε μηδ' εἰ πώποτ' ᾠκήθησαν προσελθόντ' εἶναι ῥᾴδιον εἰπεῖν· καὶ τὸ Φωκέων ἔθνος τοσοῦτον ἀνῃρημένον σιωπῶ. ἀλλὰ Θετταλία πῶς ἔχει; οὐχὶ τὰς πολιτείας καὶ τὰς πόλεις αὐτῶν παρῄρηται καὶ τετραρχίας κατέστησεν, ἵνα μὴ μόνον κατὰ πόλεις ἀλλὰ καὶ κατ' ἔθνη δουλεύωσιν; **27** αἱ δ' ἐν Εὐβοίᾳ πόλεις οὐκ ἤδη τυραννοῦνται, καὶ ταῦτ' ἐν νήσῳ πλησίον Θηβῶν καὶ Ἀθηνῶν; οὐ διαρρήδην εἰς τὰς ἐπιστολὰς γράφει "ἐμοὶ δ' ἐστὶν εἰρήνη πρὸς τοὺς ἀκούειν ἐμοῦ βουλομένους"; καὶ οὐ γράφει μὲν ταῦτα, τοῖς δ' ἔργοις οὐ ποιεῖ, ἀλλ' ἐφ' Ἑλλήσποντον οἴχεται, πρότερον ἧκεν ἐπ' Ἀμβρακίαν, Ἦλιν ἔχει τηλικαύτην πόλιν ἐν Πελοποννήσῳ, Μεγάροις ἐπεβούλευσεν πρώην, οὔθ' ἡ Ἑλλὰς οὔθ' ἡ βάρβαρος τὴν πλεονεξίαν χωρεῖ τἀνθρώπου. **28** καὶ ταῦθ' ὁρῶντες οἱ Ἕλληνες ἅπαντες καὶ ἀκούοντες οὐ πέμπομεν πρέσβεις περὶ τούτων πρὸς ἀλλήλους κἀγανακτοῦμεν, οὕτω δὲ κακῶς διακείμεθα καὶ διορωρύγμεθα κατὰ πόλεις ὥστ' ἄχρι τῆς τήμερον ἡμέρας οὐδὲν οὔτε τῶν

4

συμφερόντων οὔτε τῶν δεόντων πρᾶξαι δυνάμεθα, οὐδὲ συστῆναι, οὐδὲ κοινωνίαν βοηθείας καὶ φιλίας οὐδεμίαν ποιήσασθαι, 29 ἀλλὰ μείζω γιγνόμενον τὸν ἄνθρωπον περιορῶμεν, τὸν χρόνον κερδᾶναι τοῦτον ὃν ἄλλος ἀπόλλυται ἕκαστος ἐγνωκώς, ὥς γ' ἐμοὶ δοκεῖ, οὐχ ὅπως σωθήσεται τὰ τῶν Ἑλλήνων σκοπῶν οὐδὲ πράττων, ἐπεί, ὅτι γ' ὥσπερ περίοδος ἢ καταβολὴ πυρετοῦ ἢ ἄλλου τινὸς κακοῦ καὶ τῷ πάνυ πόρρω δοκοῦντι νῦν ἀφεστάναι προσέρχεται, οὐδεὶς ἀγνοεῖ. 30 καὶ μὴν κἀκεῖνό γ' ἴστε, ὅτι ὅσα μὲν ὑπὸ Λακεδαιμονίων ἢ ὑφ' ἡμῶν ἔπασχον οἱ Ἕλληνες, ἀλλ' οὖν ὑπὸ γνησίων γ' ὄντων τῆς Ἑλλάδος ἠδικοῦντο, καὶ τὸν αὐτὸν τρόπον ἄν τις ὑπέλαβεν τοῦθ' ὥσπερ ἂν εἰ υἱὸς ἐν οὐσίᾳ πολλῇ γεγονὼς γνήσιος διῴκει τι μὴ καλῶς μηδ' ὀρθῶς, κατ' αὐτὸ μὲν τοῦτ' ἄξιον μέμψεως εἶναι καὶ κατηγορίας, ὡς δ' οὐ προσήκων ἢ ὡς οὐ κληρονόμος τούτων ὢν ταῦτ' ἐποίει, οὐκ ἐνεῖναι λέγειν. 31 εἰ δέ γε δοῦλος ἢ ὑποβολιμαῖος τὰ μὴ προσήκοντ' ἀπώλλυε καὶ ἐλυμαίνετο, Ἡράκλεις, ὅσῳ μᾶλλον δεινὸν καὶ ὀργῆς ἄξιον πάντες ἂν ἔφησαν εἶναι. ἀλλ' οὐχ ὑπὲρ Φιλίππου καὶ ὧν ἐκεῖνος πράττει νῦν, οὐχ οὕτως ἔχουσιν, οὐ μόνον οὐχ Ἕλληνος ὄντος οὐδὲ προσήκοντος οὐδὲν τοῖς Ἕλλησιν, ἀλλ' οὐδὲ βαρβάρου ἐντεῦθεν ὅθεν καλὸν εἰπεῖν, ἀλλ' ὀλέθρου Μακεδόνος, ὅθεν οὐδ' ἀνδράποδον σπουδαῖον οὐδὲν ἦν πρότερον πρίασθαι.

32 Καίτοι τί τῆς ἐσχάτης ὕβρεως ἀπολείπει; οὐ πρὸς τῷ πόλεις ἀνῃρηκέναι τίθησι μὲν τὰ Πύθια, τὸν κοινὸν τῶν Ἑλλήνων ἀγῶνα, κἂν αὐτὸς μὴ παρῇ, τοὺς δούλους ἀγωνοθετήσοντας πέμπει; {κύριος δὲ Πυλῶν καὶ τῶν ἐπὶ τοὺς Ἕλληνας παρόδων ἐστί, καὶ φρουραῖς καὶ ξένοις τοὺς τόπους τούτους κατέχει; ἔχει δὲ καὶ τὴν προμαντείαν τοῦ θεοῦ, παρώσας ἡμᾶς καὶ Θετταλοὺς καὶ Δωριέας καὶ τοὺς ἄλλους Ἀμφικτύονας, ἧς οὐδὲ τοῖς Ἕλλησιν ἅπασι μέτεστι;} 33 γράφει δὲ Θετταλοῖς ὃν χρὴ τρόπον πολιτεύεσθαι; πέμπει δὲ ξένους τοὺς μὲν εἰς Πορθμόν, τὸν δῆμον ἐκβαλοῦντας τὸν Ἐρετριέων, τοὺς δ' ἐπ' Ὠρεόν, τύραννον Φιλιστίδην καταστήσοντας; ἀλλ' ὅμως ταῦθ' ὁρῶντες οἱ Ἕλληνες ἀνέχονται, καὶ τὸν αὐτὸν τρόπον ὥσπερ τὴν χάλαζαν ἔμοιγε δοκοῦσιν θεωρεῖν, εὐχόμενοι μὴ καθ' ἑαυτοὺς ἕκαστοι γενέσθαι, κωλύειν δ' οὐδεὶς ἐπιχειρῶν. 34 οὐ μόνον δ' ἐφ' οἷς ἡ Ἑλλὰς ὑβρίζεται ὑπ' αὐτοῦ, οὐδεὶς ἀμύνεται, ἀλλ' οὐδ' ὑπὲρ ὧν αὐτὸς ἕκαστος ἀδικεῖται· τοῦτο γὰρ ἤδη τοὔσχατόν ἐστιν. οὐ Κορινθίων ἐπ' Ἀμβρακίαν ἐλήλυθε καὶ Λευκάδα; οὐκ Ἀχαιῶν Ναύπακτον ὀμώμοκεν Αἰτωλοῖς παραδώσειν; οὐχὶ Θηβαίων Ἐχῖνον ἀφῄρηται, καὶ νῦν ἐπὶ Βυζαντίους πορεύεται συμμάχους ὄντας; 35 οὐχ ἡμῶν — ἐῶ τἆλλα — ἀλλὰ Χερρονήσου τὴν μεγίστην ἔχει πόλιν Καρδίαν; ταῦτα τοίνυν πάσχοντες ἅπαντες μέλλομεν καὶ μαλκίομεν καὶ πρὸς τοὺς πλησίον βλέπομεν, ἀπιστοῦντες ἀλλήλοις, οὐ τῷ πάντας ἡμᾶς ἀδικοῦντι. καίτοι τὸν ἅπασιν ἀσελγῶς οὕτω χρώμενον τί οἴεσθε, ἐπειδὰν καθ' ἕν' ἡμῶν ἑκάστου κύριος γένηται, τί ποιήσειν;

5

36 Τί οὖν αἴτιον τουτωνί; οὐ γὰρ ἄνευ λόγου καὶ δικαίας αἰτίας οὔτε τόθ᾽ οὕτως εἶχον ἑτοίμως πρὸς ἐλευθερίαν οἱ Ἕλληνες οὔτε νῦν πρὸς τὸ δουλεύειν. ἦν τι τότ᾽, ἦν, ὦ ἄνδρες Ἀθηναῖοι, ἐν ταῖς τῶν πολλῶν διανοίαις, ὃ νῦν οὐκ ἔστιν, ὃ καὶ τοῦ Περσῶν ἐκράτησε πλούτου καὶ ἐλευθέραν ἦγε τὴν Ἑλλάδα καὶ οὔτε ναυμαχίας οὔτε πεζῆς μάχης οὐδεμιᾶς ἡττᾶτο, νῦν δ᾽ ἀπολωλὸς ἅπαντα λελύμανται καὶ ἄνω καὶ κάτω πεποίηκε τὰ τῶν Ἑλλήνων πράγματα. **37** τί οὖν ἦν τοῦτο; {οὐδὲν ποικίλον οὐδὲ σοφόν, ἀλλ᾽ ὅτι} τοὺς παρὰ τῶν ἄρχειν βουλομένων ἢ διαφθείρειν τὴν Ἑλλάδα χρήματα λαμβάνοντας ἅπαντες ἐμίσουν, καὶ χαλεπώτατον ἦν τὸ δωροδοκοῦντ᾽ ἐλεγχθῆναι, καὶ τιμωρίᾳ μεγίστῃ τοῦτον ἐκόλαζον, {καὶ παραίτησις οὐδεμί᾽ ἦν οὐδὲ συγγνώμη.} **38** τὸν οὖν καιρὸν ἑκάστου τῶν πραγμάτων, ὃν ἡ τύχη καὶ τοῖς ἀμελοῦσιν κατὰ τῶν προσεχόντων πολλάκις παρασκευάζει, οὐκ ἦν πρίασθαι παρὰ τῶν λεγόντων οὐδὲ τῶν στρατηγούντων, οὐδὲ τὴν πρὸς ἀλλήλους ὁμόνοιαν, οὐδὲ τὴν πρὸς τοὺς τυράννους καὶ τοὺς βαρβάρους ἀπιστίαν, οὐδ᾽ ὅλως τοιοῦτον οὐδέν. **39** νῦν δ᾽ ἅπανθ᾽ ὥσπερ ἐξ ἀγορᾶς ἐκπέπραται ταῦτα, ἀντεισῆκται δ᾽ ἀντὶ τούτων ὑφ᾽ ὧν ἀπόλωλε καὶ νενόσηκεν ἡ Ἑλλάς. ταῦτα δ᾽ ἐστὶ τί; ζῆλος, εἴ τις εἴληφέ τι· γέλως, ἂν ὁμολογῇ· {συγγνώμη τοῖς ἐλεγχομένοις·} μῖσος, ἂν τούτοις τις ἐπιτιμᾷ· τἆλλα πάνθ᾽ ὅσ᾽ ἐκ τοῦ δωροδοκεῖν ἤρτηται. **40** ἐπεὶ τριήρεις γε καὶ σωμάτων πλῆθος καὶ χρημάτων καὶ τῆς ἄλλης κατασκευῆς ἀφθονία, καὶ τἆλλ᾽ οἷς ἄν τις ἰσχύειν τὰς πόλεις κρίνοι, νῦν ἅπασι καὶ πλείω καὶ μείζω ἐστὶ τῶν τότε πολλῷ. ἀλλὰ ταῦτ᾽ ἄχρηστα, ἄπρακτα, ἀνόνητα ὑπὸ τῶν πωλούντων γίγνεται.

41 Ὅτι δ᾽ οὕτω ταῦτ᾽ ἔχει τὰ μὲν νῦν ὁρᾶτε δήπου καὶ οὐδὲν ἐμοῦ προσδεῖσθε μάρτυρος· τὰ δ᾽ ἐν τοῖς ἄνωθεν χρόνοις ὅτι τἀναντί᾽ εἶχεν ἐγὼ δηλώσω, οὐ λόγους ἐμαυτοῦ λέγων, ἀλλὰ γράμματα τῶν προγόνων τῶν ὑμετέρων ἀκεῖνοι κατέθεντ᾽ εἰς στήλην χαλκῆν γράψαντες εἰς ἀκρόπολιν, {οὐχ ἵν᾽ αὐτοῖς ᾖ χρήσιμα (καὶ γὰρ ἄνευ τούτων τῶν γραμμάτων τὰ δέοντ᾽ ἐφρόνουν), ἀλλ᾽ ἵν᾽ ὑμεῖς ἔχηθ᾽ ὑπομνήματα καὶ παραδείγματα ὡς ὑπὲρ τῶν τοιούτων σπουδάζειν προσήκει. τί οὖν λέγει τὰ γράμματα;} **42** "Ἄρθμιος" φησὶ "Πυθώνακτος Ζελείτης ἄτιμος καὶ πολέμιος τοῦ δήμου τοῦ Ἀθηναίων καὶ τῶν συμμάχων αὐτὸς καὶ γένος." εἶθ᾽ ἡ αἰτία γέγραπται, δι᾽ ἣν ταῦτ᾽ ἐγένετο· "ὅτι τὸν χρυσὸν τὸν ἐκ Μήδων εἰς Πελοπόννησον ἤγαγεν." ταῦτ᾽ ἐστὶ τὰ γράμματα. **43** λογίζεσθε δὴ πρὸς θεῶν, τίς ἦν ποθ᾽ ἡ διάνοια τῶν Ἀθηναίων τῶν τότε, ταῦτα ποιούντων, ἢ τί τὸ ἀξίωμα. ἐκεῖνοι Ζελείτην τινά, Ἄρθμιον, δοῦλον βασιλέως (ἡ γὰρ Ζέλειά ἐστι τῆς Ἀσίας), ὅτι τῷ δεσπότῃ διακονῶν χρυσίον ἤγαγεν εἰς Πελοπόννησον, οὐκ Ἀθήναζε, ἐχθρὸν αὐτῶν ἀνέγραψαν καὶ τῶν συμμάχων αὐτὸν καὶ γένος, καὶ ἀτίμους. **44** τοῦτο δ᾽ ἐστὶν οὐχ ἣν οὑτωσί τις ἂν φήσειεν ἀτιμίαν· τί γὰρ τῷ Ζελείτῃ, τῶν Ἀθηναίων κοινῶν εἰ μὴ μεθέξειν ἔμελλεν; ἀλλ᾽ ἐν τοῖς φονικοῖς γέγραπται νόμοις, ὑπὲρ ὧν ἂν μὴ διδῷ φόνου δικάσασθαι, {ἀλλ᾽ εὐαγὲς ᾖ τὸ ἀποκτεῖναι,} "καὶ ἄτιμος" φησὶ "τεθνάτω." τοῦτο δὴ λέγει, καθαρὸν τὸν τούτων τιν' ἀποκτείναντ' εἶναι. **45** οὐκοῦν ἐνόμιζον ἐκεῖνοι τῆς πάντων τῶν Ἑλλήνων σωτηρίας αὐτοῖς ἐπιμελητέον εἶναι· οὐ γὰρ ἂν αὐτοῖς ἔμελ' εἴ τις ἐν Πελοποννήσῳ τινὰς ὠνεῖται καὶ διαφθείρει, μὴ τοῦθ' ὑπολαμβάνουσιν· ἐκόλαζον δ' οὕτω καὶ ἐτιμωροῦνθ' οὓς αἴσθοιντο, ὥστε καὶ στηλίτας ποιεῖν. ἐκ δὲ τούτων εἰκότως τὰ τῶν Ἑλλήνων ἦν τῷ βαρβάρῳ φοβερά, οὐχ ὁ βάρβαρος τοῖς Ἕλλησιν. **46** ἀλλ' οὐ νῦν· οὐ γὰρ οὕτως ἔχεθ' ὑμεῖς οὔτε πρὸς τὰ τοιαῦτ' οὔτε πρὸς τἆλλα, ἀλλὰ πῶς; (ἴστ' αὐτοί· τί γὰρ δεῖ περὶ πάντων ὑμῶν κατηγορεῖν; παραπλησίως δὲ καὶ οὐδὲν βέλτιον ὑμῶν ἅπαντες οἱ λοιποὶ Ἕλληνες· διόπερ φήμ' ἔγωγε καὶ σπουδῆς πολλῆς καὶ βουλῆς ἀγαθῆς τὰ παρόντα πράγματα προσδεῖσθαι. τίνος;) εἴπω κελεύετε; καὶ οὐκ ὀργιεῖσθε;

[ΕΚ ΤΟΥ ΓΡΑΜΜΑΤΕΙΟΥ ΑΝΑΓΙΓΝΩΣΚΕΙ]

47 Ἔστι τοίνυν τις εὐήθης λόγος παρὰ τῶν παραμυθεῖσθαι βουλομένων τὴν πόλιν, ὡς ἄρ' οὔπω Φίλιππός ἐστιν οἷοί ποτ' ἦσαν Λακεδαιμόνιοι, οἳ θαλάττης μὲν ἦρχον καὶ γῆς ἁπάσης, βασιλέα δὲ σύμμαχον εἶχον, ὑφίστατο δ' οὐδὲν αὐτούς· ἀλλ' ὅμως ἠμύνατο κἀκείνους ἡ πόλις καὶ οὐκ ἀνηρπάσθη. ἐγὼ δ' ἁπάντων ὡς ἔπος εἰπεῖν πολλὴν εἰληφότων ἐπίδοσιν, καὶ οὐδὲν ὁμοίων ὄντων τῶν νῦν τοῖς πρότερον, οὐδὲν ἡγοῦμαι πλέον ἢ τὰ τοῦ πολέμου κεκινῆσθαι κἀπιδεδωκέναι. **48** πρῶτον μὲν γὰρ ἀκούω Λακεδαιμονίους τότε καὶ πάντας τοὺς ἄλλους, τέτταρας μῆνας ἢ πέντε, τὴν ὡραίαν αὐτήν, ἐμβαλόντας ἂν καὶ κακώσαντας τὴν χώραν ὁπλίταις καὶ πολιτικοῖς στρατεύμασιν ἀναχωρεῖν ἐπ' οἴκου πάλιν· οὕτω δ' ἀρχαίως εἶχον, μᾶλλον δὲ πολιτικῶς, ὥστ' οὐδὲ χρημάτων ὠνεῖσθαι παρ' οὐδενὸς οὐδέν, ἀλλ' εἶναι νόμιμόν τινα καὶ προφανῆ τὸν πόλεμον. **49** νυνὶ δ' ὁρᾶτε μὲν δήπου τὰ πλεῖστα τοὺς προδότας ἀπολωλεκότας, οὐδὲν δ' ἐκ παρατάξεως οὐδὲ μάχης γιγνόμενον· ἀκούετε δὲ Φίλιππον οὐχὶ τῷ φάλαγγ' ὁπλιτῶν ἄγειν βαδίζονθ' ὅποι βούλεται, ἀλλὰ τῷ ψιλούς, ἱππέας, τοξότας, ξένους, τοιοῦτον ἐξηρτῆσθαι στρατόπεδον. **50** ἐπειδὰν δ' ἐπὶ τούτοις πρὸς νοσοῦντας ἐν αὑτοῖς προσπέσῃ καὶ μηδεὶς ὑπὲρ τῆς χώρας δι' ἀπιστίαν ἐξίῃ, μηχανήματ' ἐπιστήσας πολιορκεῖ. καὶ σιωπῶ θέρος καὶ χειμῶνα, ὡς οὐδὲν διαφέρει, οὐδ' ἔστιν ἐξαίρετος ὥρα τις ἣν διαλείπει. **51** ταῦτα μέντοι πάντας εἰδότας καὶ λογιζομένους οὐ δεῖ προσέσθαι τὸν πόλεμον εἰς τὴν χώραν, οὐδ' εἰς τὴν εὐήθειαν τὴν τοῦ τότε πρὸς Λακεδαιμονίους πολέμου βλέποντας ἐκτραχηλισθῆναι, ἀλλ' ὡς ἐκ πλείστου φυλάττεσθαι τοῖς πράγμασι καὶ ταῖς παρασκευαῖς, ὅπως οἴκοθεν μὴ κινήσεται σκοπούντας, οὐχὶ συμπλακέντας διαγωνίζεσθαι. **52** πρὸς μὲν γὰρ πόλεμον πολλὰ φύσει πλεονεκτήμαθ' ἡμῖν ὑπάρχει, ἄν περ, ὦ ἄνδρες Ἀθηναῖοι, ποιεῖν ἐθέλωμεν ἃ δεῖ, ἡ φύσις τῆς ἐκείνου χώρας, ἧς ἄγειν καὶ φέρειν ἔστι πολλὴν καὶ κακῶς ποιεῖν, ἄλλα μυρία· εἰς δ' ἀγῶνα ἄμεινον ἡμῶν ἐκεῖνος ἤσκηται.

53 Οὐ μόνον δὲ δεῖ ταῦτα γιγνώσκειν, οὐδὲ τοῖς ἔργοις ἐκεῖνον ἀμύνεσθαι τοῖς τοῦ πολέμου, ἀλλὰ καὶ τῷ λογισμῷ καὶ τῇ διανοίᾳ τοὺς παρ' ὑμῖν ὑπὲρ αὐτοῦ λέγοντας μισῆσαι, ἐνθυμουμένους ὅτι οὐκ ἔνεστι τῶν τῆς πόλεως ἐχθρῶν κρατῆσαι, πρὶν ἂν τοὺς ἐν αὐτῇ τῇ πόλει κολάσηθ' ὑπηρετοῦντας ἐκείνοις. **54** ὃ μὰ τὸν Δία καὶ τοὺς ἄλλους θεοὺς οὐ δυνήσεσθ' ὑμεῖς ποιῆσαι, ἀλλ' εἰς τοῦτ' ἀφῖχθε μωρίας ἢ παρανοίας ἢ οὐκ ἔχω τί λέγω (πολλάκις γὰρ ἔμοιγ' ἐπελήλυθε καὶ τοῦτο φοβεῖσθαι, μή τι δαιμόνιον τὰ πράγματ' ἐλαύνῃ), ὥστε λοιδορίας, φθόνου, σκώμματος, ἧστινος ἂν τύχηθ' ἕνεκ' αἰτίας ἀνθρώπους μισθωτούς, ὧν οὐδ' ἂν ἀρνηθεῖεν ἔνιοι ὡς οὐκ εἰσὶ τοιοῦτοι, λέγειν κελεύετε, καὶ γελᾶτε, ἄν τισι λοιδορηθῶσιν. **55** καὶ οὐχί πω τοῦτο δεινόν, καίπερ ὂν δεινόν· ἀλλὰ καὶ μετὰ πλείονος ἀσφαλείας πολιτεύεσθαι δεδώκατε τούτοις ἢ τοῖς ὑπὲρ ὑμῶν λέγουσιν. καίτοι θεάσασθ' ὅσας συμφορὰς παρασκευάζει τὸ τῶν τοιούτων ἐθέλειν ἀκροᾶσθαι. λέξω δ' ἔργα, ἃ πάντες εἴσεσθε.

56 Ἦσαν ἐν Ὀλύνθῳ τῶν ἐν τοῖς πράγμασι τινὲς μὲν Φιλίππου καὶ πάνθ' ὑπηρετοῦντες ἐκείνῳ, τινὲς δὲ τοῦ βελτίστου καὶ ὅπως μὴ δουλεύσουσιν οἱ πολῖται πράττοντες. πότεροι δὴ τὴν πατρίδ' ἐξώλεσαν; ἢ πότεροι τοὺς ἱππέας προὔδοσαν, ὧν προδοθέντων Ὄλυνθος ἀπώλετο; οἱ τὰ Φιλίππου φρονοῦντες, καὶ ὅτ' ἦν ἡ πόλις τοὺς τὰ βέλτιστα λέγοντας συκοφαντοῦντες καὶ διαβάλλοντες οὕτως, ὥστε τόν γ' Ἀπολλωνίδην καὶ ἐκβαλεῖν ὁ δῆμος ὁ τῶν Ὀλυνθίων ἐπείσθη.

57 Οὐ τοίνυν παρὰ τούτοις μόνον τὸ ἔθος τοῦτο πάντα κάκ' εἰργάσατο, ἄλλοθι δ' οὐδαμοῦ· ἀλλ' ἐν Ἐρετρίᾳ, ἐπειδὴ ἀπαλλαγέντος Πλουτάρχου καὶ τῶν ξένων ὁ δῆμος εἶχε τὴν πόλιν καὶ τὸν Πορθμόν, οἱ μὲν ἐφ' ὑμᾶς ἦγον τὰ πράγματα, οἱ δ' ἐπὶ Φίλιππον. ἀκούοντες δὲ τούτων τὰ πολλά, μᾶλλον δὲ τὰ πάνθ' οἱ ταλαίπωροι καὶ δυστυχεῖς Ἐρετριεῖς, τελευτῶντες ἐπείσθησαν τοὺς ὑπὲρ αὑτῶν λέγοντας ἐκβαλεῖν. **58** καὶ γάρ τοι πέμψας Ἱππόνικον ὁ σύμμαχος αὐτοῖς Φίλιππος καὶ ξένους χιλίους, τὰ τείχη περιεῖλε τοῦ Πορθμοῦ καὶ τρεῖς κατέστησε τυράννους, Ἵππαρχον, Αὐτομέδοντα, Κλείταρχον. καὶ μετὰ ταῦτ' ἐξελήλακεν ἐκ τῆς χώρας δὶς ἤδη βουλομένους σῴζεσθαι {,τότε μὲν πέμψας τοὺς μετ' Εὐρυλόχου ξένους, πάλιν δὲ τοὺς μετὰ Παρμενίωνος}.

59 Καὶ τί δεῖ τὰ πολλὰ λέγειν; ἀλλ' ἐν Ὠρεῷ Φιλιστίδης μὲν ἔπραττε Φιλίππῳ καὶ Μένιππος καὶ Σωκράτης καὶ Θόας καὶ Ἀγαπαῖος, οἵπερ νῦν ἔχουσι τὴν πόλιν (καὶ ταῦτ' ᾔδεσαν ἅπαντες), Εὔφραιος δέ τις ἄνθρωπος καὶ παρ' ἡμῖν ποτ' ἐνθάδ' οἰκήσας, ὅπως ἐλεύθεροι καὶ μηδενὸς δοῦλοι ἔσονται. **60** οὗτος τὰ μὲν ἄλλ' ὡς ὑβρίζετο καὶ προὐπηλακίζεθ' ὑπὸ τοῦ δήμου, πόλλ' ἂν εἴη λέγειν· ἐνιαυτῷ δὲ πρότερον τῆς ἁλώσεως ἐνέδειξεν ὡς προδότην τὸν Φιλιστίδην καὶ τοὺς μετ' αὐτοῦ, αἰσθόμενος ἃ πράττουσιν. συστραφέντες δ' ἄνθρωποι πολλοὶ καὶ χορηγὸν ἔχοντες Φίλιππον καὶ πρυτανευόμενοι ἀπάγουσι τὸν Εὐφραῖον

KATA ΦΙΛΙΠΠΟΥ Γ

εἰς τὸ δεσμωτήριον, ὡς συνταράττοντα τὴν πόλιν. 61 ὁρῶν δὲ ταῦθ' ὁ δῆμος ὁ τῶν Ὠρειτῶν, ἀντὶ τοῦ τῷ μὲν βοηθεῖν, τοὺς δ' ἀποτυμπανίσαι, τοῖς μὲν οὐκ ὠργίζετο, τὸν δ' ἐπιτήδειον ταῦτα παθεῖν ἔφη καὶ ἐπέχαιρεν. μετὰ ταῦθ' οἱ μὲν ἐπ' ἐξουσίας ὁπόσης ἐβούλοντ' ἔπραττον ὅπως ἡ πόλις ληφθήσεται, καὶ κατεσκευάζοντο τὴν πρᾶξιν· τῶν δὲ πολλῶν εἴ τις αἴσθοιτο, ἐσίγα καὶ κατεπέπληκτο, τὸν Εὔφραῖον οἷ' ἔπαθεν μεμνημένοι. οὕτω δ' ἀθλίως διέκειντο, ὥστ' οὐ πρότερον ἐτόλμησεν οὐδεὶς τοιούτου κακοῦ προσιόντος ῥῆξαι φωνήν, πρὶν διασκευασάμενοι πρὸς τὰ τείχη προσῇεσαν οἱ πολέμιοι· τηνικαῦτα δ' οἱ μὲν ἠμύνοντο, οἱ δὲ προὐδίδοσαν. 62 τῆς πόλεως δ' οὕτως ἁλούσης αἰσχρῶς καὶ κακῶς οἱ μὲν ἄρχουσι καὶ τυραννοῦσι, τοὺς τότε σῴζοντας ἑαυτοὺς καὶ τὸν Εὔφραῖον ἑτοίμους ὁτιοῦν ποιεῖν ὄντας τοὺς μὲν ἐκβαλόντες, τοὺς δ' ἀποκτείναντες, ὁ δ' Εὔφραῖος ἐκεῖνος ἀπέσφαξεν ἑαυτόν, ἔργῳ μαρτυρήσας ὅτι καὶ δικαίως καὶ καθαρῶς ὑπὲρ τῶν πολιτῶν ἀνθειστήκει Φιλίππῳ.

63 Τί οὖν ποτ' αἴτιον, θαυμάζετ' ἴσως, τὸ καὶ τοὺς Ὀλυνθίους καὶ τοὺς Ἐρετριέας καὶ τοὺς Ὠρείτας ἥδιον πρὸς τοὺς ὑπὲρ Φιλίππου λέγοντας ἔχειν ἢ τοὺς ὑπὲρ αὑτῶν; ὅπερ καὶ παρ' ὑμῖν, ὅτι τοῖς μὲν ὑπὲρ τοῦ βελτίστου λέγουσιν οὐδὲ βουλομένοις ἔνεστιν ἐνίοτε πρὸς χάριν οὐδὲν εἰπεῖν· τὰ γὰρ πράγματ' ἀνάγκη σκοπεῖν ὅπως σωθήσεται· οἱ δ' ἐν αὐτοῖς οἷς χαρίζονται Φιλίππῳ συμπράττουσιν. 64 εἰσφέρειν ἐκέλευον, οἱ δ' οὐδὲν δεῖν ἔφασαν· πολεμεῖν καὶ μὴ πιστεύειν, οἱ δ' ἄγειν εἰρήνην, ἕως ἐγκατελήφθησαν. τἆλλα τὸν αὐτὸν τρόπον οἶμαι πάνθ', ἵνα μὴ καθ' ἕκαστα λέγω· οἱ μὲν ἐφ' οἷς χαριοῦνται, ταῦτ' ἔλεγον, οἱ δ' ἐξ ὧν ἔμελλον σωθήσεσθαι. πολλὰ δὲ καὶ τὰ τελευταῖα οὐχ οὕτως πρὸς χάριν οὐδὲ δι' ἄγνοιαν οἱ πολλοὶ προσίεντο, ἀλλ' ὑποκατακλινόμενοι, ἐπειδὴ τοῖς ὅλοις ἡττᾶσθαι ἐνόμιζον. 65 ὃ νὴ τὸν Δία καὶ τὸν Ἀπόλλω δέδοικ' ἐγὼ μὴ πάθηθ' ὑμεῖς, ἐπειδὰν εἰδῆτ' ἐκλογιζόμενοι μηδὲν ἔθ' ὑμῖν ἐνόν. καίτοι μὴ γένοιτο μέν, ὦ ἄνδρες Ἀθηναῖοι, τὰ πράγματ' ἐν τούτῳ· τεθνάναι δὲ μυριάκις κρεῖττον ἢ κολακείᾳ τι ποιῆσαι Φιλίππου {καὶ προέσθαι τῶν ὑπὲρ ὑμῶν λεγόντων τινάς}. καλήν γ' οἱ πολλοὶ νῦν ἀπειλήφασιν Ὠρειτῶν χάριν, ὅτι τοῖς Φιλίππου φίλοις ἐπέτρεψαν αὑτούς, τὸν δ' Εὔφραῖον ἐώθουν· 66 καλήν γ' ὁ δῆμος ὁ Ἐρετριέων, ὅτι τοὺς ὑμετέρους πρέσβεις ἀπήλασεν, Κλειτάρχῳ δ' ἐνέδωκεν αὑτόν· δουλεύουσί γε μαστιγούμενοι καὶ σφαττόμενοι. καλῶς Ὀλυνθίων ἐφείσατο τῶν τὸν μὲν Λασθένην ἵππαρχον χειροτονησάντων, τὸν δ' Ἀπολλωνίδην ἐκβαλόντων. 67 μωρία καὶ κακία τὰ τοιαῦτ' ἐλπίζειν, καὶ κακῶς βουλευομένους καὶ μηδὲν ὧν προσήκει ποιεῖν ἐθέλοντας, ἀλλὰ τῶν ὑπὲρ τῶν ἐχθρῶν λεγόντων ἀκροωμένους, τηλικαύτην ἡγεῖσθαι πόλιν οἰκεῖν τὸ μέγεθος ὥστε <μηδέν>, μηδ' ἂν ὁτιοῦν ᾖ, δεινὸν πείσεσθαι. 68 καὶ μὴν ἐκεῖνό γ' αἰσχρόν, ὕστερόν ποτ' εἰπεῖν "τίς γὰρ ἂν ᾠήθη ταῦτα γενέσθαι; νὴ τὸν Δί', ἔδει γὰρ τὸ καὶ τὸ ποιῆσαι καὶ τὸ μὴ ποιῆσαι." πόλλ' ἂν εἰπεῖν ἔχοιεν Ὀλύνθιοι νῦν, ἃ τότ' εἰ προείδοντο, οὐκ ἂν ἀπώλοντο· πόλλ' ἂν Ὠρεῖται, πολλὰ Φωκεῖς, πολλὰ τῶν ἀπολωλότων ἕκαστοι. 69 ἀλλὰ τί τούτων ὄφελος αὐτοῖς; ἕως ἂν

9

σῴζηται τὸ σκάφος, ἄν τε μεῖζον ἄν τ' ἔλαττον ᾖ, τότε χρὴ καὶ ναύτην καὶ κυβερνήτην καὶ πάντ' ἄνδρ' ἑξῆς προθύμους εἶναι, καὶ ὅπως μήθ' ἑκὼν μήτ' ἄκων μηδεὶς ἀνατρέψει, τοῦτο σκοπεῖσθαι· ἐπειδὰν δ' ἡ θάλαττα ὑπέρσχῃ, μάταιος ἡ σπουδή. **70** καὶ ἡμεῖς τοίνυν, ὦ ἄνδρες Ἀθηναῖοι, ἕως ἐσμὲν σῷοι, πόλιν μεγίστην ἔχοντες, ἀφορμὰς πλείστας, ἀξίωμα κάλλιστον, τί ποιῶμεν; πάλαι τις ἡδέως ἂν ἴσως ἐρωτήσας κάθηται. ἐγὼ νὴ Δί' ἐρῶ, καὶ γράψω δέ, ὥστ' ἂν βούλησθε χειροτονήσετε. αὐτοὶ πρῶτον ἀμυνόμενοι καὶ παρασκευαζόμενοι, τριήρεσι καὶ χρήμασι καὶ στρατιώταις λέγω· καὶ γὰρ ἂν ἅπαντες δήπου δουλεύειν συγχωρήσωσιν οἱ ἄλλοι, ἡμῖν γ' ὑπὲρ τῆς ἐλευθερίας ἀγωνιστέον· **71** ταῦτα δὴ πάντ' αὐτοὶ παρεσκευασμένοι καὶ ποιήσαντες φανερὰ τοὺς ἄλλους ἤδη παρακαλῶμεν, καὶ τοὺς ταῦτα διδάξοντας ἐκπέμπωμεν πρέσβεις {πανταχοῖ, εἰς Πελοπόννησον, εἰς· Ρόδον, εἰς Χίον, ὡς βασιλέα λέγω (οὐδὲ γὰρ τῶν ἐκείνῳ συμφερόντων ἀφέστηκε τὸ μὴ τοῦτον ἐᾶσαι πάντα καταστρέψασθαι)}, ἵν' ἐὰν μὲν πείσητε, κοινωνοὺς ἔχητε καὶ τῶν κινδύνων καὶ τῶν ἀναλωμάτων, ἄν τι δέῃ, εἰ δὲ μή, χρόνους γ' ἐμποιῆτε τοῖς πράγμασιν. **72** ἐπειδὴ γάρ ἐστι πρὸς ἄνδρα καὶ οὐχὶ συνεστώσης πόλεως ἰσχὺν ὁ πόλεμος, οὐδὲ τοῦτ' ἄχρηστον, οὐδ' αἱ πέρυσιν πρεσβεῖαι περὶ τὴν Πελοπόννησον ἐκεῖναι καὶ κατηγορίαι, ἃς ἐγὼ καὶ Πολύευκτος ὁ βέλτιστος ἐκεινοσὶ καὶ Ἡγήσιππος καὶ οἱ ἄλλοι πρέσβεις περιήλθομεν, καὶ ἐποιήσαμεν ἐπισχεῖν ἐκεῖνον καὶ μήτ' ἐπ' Ἀμβρακίαν ἐλθεῖν μήτ' εἰς Πελοπόννησον ὁρμῆσαι. **73** οὐ μέντοι λέγω μηδὲν αὐτοὺς ὑπὲρ αὑτῶν ἀναγκαῖον ἐθέλοντας ποιεῖν, τοὺς ἄλλους παρακαλεῖν· καὶ γὰρ εὔηθες τὰ οἰκεῖ' αὐτοὺς προϊεμένους τῶν ἀλλοτρίων φάσκειν κήδεσθαι, καὶ τὰ παρόντα περιορῶντας ὑπὲρ τῶν μελλόντων τοὺς ἄλλους φοβεῖν. οὐ λέγω ταῦτα, ἀλλὰ τοῖς μὲν ἐν Χερρονήσῳ χρήματ' ἀποστέλλειν φημὶ δεῖν καὶ τἄλλ' ὅσ' ἀξιοῦσι ποιεῖν, αὐτοὺς δὲ παρασκευάζεσθαι, τοὺς δ' ἄλλους Ἕλληνας συγκαλεῖν, συνάγειν, διδάσκειν, νουθετεῖν· ταῦτ' ἐστὶ πόλεως ἀξίωμ' ἐχούσης ἡλίκον ὑμῖν ὑπάρχει. **74** εἰ δ' οἴεσθε Χαλκιδέας τὴν Ἑλλάδα σώσειν ἢ Μεγαρέας, ὑμεῖς δ' ἀποδράσεσθαι τὰ πράγματα, οὐκ ὀρθῶς οἴεσθε· ἀγαπητὸν γὰρ ἐὰν αὐτοὶ σῴζωνται τούτων ἕκαστοι. ἀλλ' ὑμῖν τοῦτο πρακτέον· ὑμῖν οἱ πρόγονοι τοῦτο τὸ γέρας ἐκτήσαντο καὶ κατέλιπον μετὰ πολλῶν καὶ μεγάλων κινδύνων. **75** εἰ δ' ὃ βούλεται ζητῶν ἕκαστος καθεδεῖται καὶ ὅπως μηδὲν αὐτὸς ποιήσει σκοπῶν, πρῶτον μὲν οὐδὲ μήποθ' εὕρῃ τοὺς ποιήσοντας, ἔπειτα δέδοιχ' ὅπως μὴ πάνθ' ἅμ' ὅσ' οὐ βουλόμεθα ποιεῖν ἡμῖν ἀνάγκη γενήσεται.

76 Ἐγὼ μὲν δὴ ταῦτα λέγω, ταῦτα γράφω· καὶ οἴομαι καὶ νῦν ἔτ' ἐπανορθωθῆναι ἂν τὰ πράγματα τούτων γιγνομένων. εἰ δέ τις ἔχει τούτων τι βέλτιον, λεγέτω καὶ συμβουλευέτω. ὅ τι δ' ὑμῖν δόξει, τοῦτ', ὦ πάντες θεοί, συνενέγκοι.

MORPHOLOGY AND SYNTAX

The following few pages, to which constant reference is made in the running commentary, focus on certain aspects of word-formation and syntactical structures. If you have an imperfect grasp of any of the areas covered, you will find it beneficial to study the data presented in the relevant section or sections *before* you embark on the text itself.

A. THE PERFECT AND PLUPERFECT

A.1

In Beginners' courses, the perfect and pluperfect generally crop up at a late stage, when there is mounting pressure to reach the the final lesson. The former at any rate can prove a real distraction among other more general difficulties commonly encountered when an extended Greek text is tackled seriously for the first time. In fact, the perfect systems do not lend themselves to total assimilation within a very short time-span: one needs to work one's way into them, and to do that one has got to read a fair bit of Greek. A few moments spent (preferably with a set of paradigms illustrating the basic types by your side) on reviewing the perfects and pluperfects that actually occur in this speech may prove useful.

A.2.a

The important perfect εἰδέναι "to know" (from the same root as ὁρᾶν, the aorist of εἶδον) is so eccentric that it is better considered separately. We find:

Indicative 1st person singular οἶδ(α); 2nd person plural ἴστε
Subjunctive 2nd person plural εἰδῆτ(ε)
Participle εἰδότας
— Past tense (~ pluperfect):
3rd person plural ἤδεσαν

A.2.b

It is convenient to consider at this point the verb κεῖσθαι ("to have been put", "to lie (down)"), since it serves as the *perfect passive* of τιθέναι ("to put"); it occurs in compounded form:

Indicative 1st plural διακείμεθα; 2nd plural διάκεισθε
— Past tense:
3rd singular διέκειτο; 3rd plural διέκειντο

A.3.a

— Active with *reduplication:*

Indicative 1st singular δέδοικ(α) (3x) (δεδοικέναι, a perfect in the sense "to be afraid", "to fear"); 3rd singular συμ-βέβηκεν (συμ-βαίνειν), κεκράτηκε(ν) (2x) (κρατεῖν), νενόσηκεν (νοσεῖν), πεποίηκε (2x) (ποιεῖν); 2nd plural δεδώκατε (διδόναι) & μετα-δεδώκατε; 3rd plural γεγόνασιν (γίγνεσθαι, active version) Infinitive πεπομφέναι (πέμπειν), ἐπι-δεδωκέναι (ἐπι-διδόναι) Participle γεγονώς & γεγονυίας (γίγνεσθαι, cf. above)

— Active with *modified reduplication:*

Participle συγ-κεχωρηκότας (συγ-χωρεῖν) Infinitive/ 3rd singular Imperative τεθνάναι ("to be dead", sometimes "to die")/ τεθνάτω ((ἀπο-)θνῄσκειν)

— Active with *'Attic' reduplication*[1]:

(i) From ἐξ-ελαύνειν: Indicative 3rd singular ἐξ-ελήλακεν; 2nd plural ἐξ-εληλάκατε (ii) From (-)ἰέναι/ (-)ἔρχομαι: Indicative 3rd singular ἐλήλυθε/ ἐπ-ελήλυθε Participle παρ-εληλυθόσι (iii) From ἀπ-ολλύναι: Indicative 3rd singular ἀπ-όλωλε Participle ἀπ-ολωλεκότας, and also (second perfect, = "perish" sim.) ἀπ-ολωλός/ -ολωλότων (iv) From ὀμνύναι: Indicative 3rd singular ὀμώμοκεν

A.3.b

— Active with *(modified) augmentation/ irregularities:*

The two commonest in this category are:

(i) From ἱστάναι in compounded form: Indicative 1st singular ἀφ-έστηκα Participle καθεστηκότ(α) and "second perfect" Infinitive ἀφ-εστάναι Participle καθ-εστώτων & συν-εστώσης (ii) λαμβάνειν and compounds: Indicative 3rd singular εἴληφε/ προ-είληφε; 3rd plural ἀπ-ειλήφασιν Participle εἰληφότων

In addition:

Indicative 3rd singular ἠδίκηκε (ἀδικεῖν), ἀν-ῄρηκεν (ἀν-αιρεῖν); 3rd plural ἐγνώκασιν (γιγνώσκειν) Infinitive ἀν-ῃρηκέναι Participle ἐγνωκώς

12

MORPHOLOGY AND SYNTAX

A.4.a

— Middle-Passive with *reduplication:*
Indicative 3rd singular γέγραπται (2x) (γράφειν), λελύμανται (λυμαίνεσθαι), ἐκ-πέπραται (ἐκ-πιπράσκειν); 2nd plural κεκίνησθε (κινεῖν)
Infinitive κεκινῆσθαι, τετυφῶσθαι (τυφοῦν)
Participle μεμνημένοι (μεμνῆσθαι, perfect in the sense "to recall, remember")
— Middle-Passive with *'Attic' reduplication*[1]:
Indicative 1st plural δι-ορωρύγμεθα (δι-ορύττειν)

A.4.b

— Middle-Passive with *(modified) augmentation/ irregularities:*
Indicative 2nd plural ἀφ-ῖχθε (ἀφ-ικνεῖσθαι), otherwise 3rd singular: ἀντ-εισ-ῆκται (ἀντ-εισ-άγειν), ἐξ-ημάρτηται (ἐξ-αμαρτάνειν), ηὔξηται (αὐξάνειν/ αὔξειν); ἤρτηται (ἀρτᾶν); ἤσκηται (ἀσκεῖν), and ἀφ-ῄρηται/ παρ-ῄρηται (ἀφ-αιρεῖσθαι/ παρ-αιρεῖσθαι), ἀφ-ῖκται (ἀφ-ικνεῖσθαι); προ-εῖται (προ-ιέναι/ -ίημι)
Infinitive ἐξ-ηρτῆσθαι (ἐξ-αρτᾶν)
Participle ὑπ-ηγμένα (ὑπ-άγειν), ἀπ-εσταλμένων (ἀπο-στέλλειν), παρ-εσκευασμένοι (παρα-σκευάζεσθαι); ἠδικημένων (ἀδικεῖν), ἀν-ῃρημένον (ἀν-αιρεῖν); προ-ειμένα (προ-ιέναι/ -ίημι)

A.5

The past of the perfect, the pluperfect, occurs twice in the active (3rd singular ἀνθ-ειστήκει from ἀνθ-ιστάναι, and, with 'Attic' reduplication[1], ὠμωμόκει from ὀμνύναι); and once in the passive (3rd singular κατ-επέπληκτο, from κατα-πλήττεσθαι).

[1] Where a verb beginning with a vowel reduplicates the initial vowel *and* consonant and lengthens the vowel that follows reduplication.

B. ARTICULAR INFINITIVE

B.1

The neuter singular of the definite article is a natural ally of the infinitive, which functions as a verbal noun. So τὸ νικᾶν, "the act of winning", "the attainment of victory", "the capacity/ tendency to win" etc., in negative form τὸ μὴ νικᾶν, "non-attainment of victory", "failure/ inability to win" etc.

B.2

Tenses. Of the 18 examples in the speech, 10 are present active, 1 present middle, 2 aorist active, 1 aorist middle, 2 aorist passive, 1 perfect active, 1 perfect passive. Thus §22 τὸ ποιεῖν ὅτι βούλεται, "the ability/ freedom to do what he wants", §32 πρὸς τῷ πόλεις ἀνῃρηκέναι, "in addition to his having wiped out cities", etc.

13

B.3

Flexibility. The articular infinitive is used in the nominative as subject of the sentence (§§22 four times, 37, 55), in the accusative (of relation) (§63), as a dative of means/ respect (§§18 three times, 49 twice), in cases governed by various prepositions (accusative §36, genitive §§3, 39, 61 twice, dative §32).

B.4

The infinitival element in its turn can govern accusative (§18 and often), dative (§61), infinitive (§55); with dependent clause §22.

B.5

The subject of the infinitive, where it differs from the subject of the leading verb, is expressed by the accusative: §§18 three times, 22, 37, 63.

C. SYNTAX OF THE SUBJUNCTIVE

C.1

This section reviews all the uses to which the subjunctive is put in the course of the speech.

C.2

In this speech the subjunctive is used most commonly with ἐάν i.e. εἰ + ἄν (6x), alternative form ἄν [ἄ] (15x), with crasis κἄν (2x), negative μή:

(a) To express a prospective condition, type "[*protasis*]If you do so [viz. at some point in the future], [*apodosis*] you will be punished". The verb of the apodosis is future indicative in §§2, 70, but other kinds of leading verb are possible too (notably present indicative §§3, 4 etc.).

(b) A general condition or supposition (in practice sometimes difficult to distinguish from the foregoing), type "If somebody [in cases in which a person] acts thus, the law stipulates [as a general principle] imposition of the death-penalty". See e.g. the two examples in §39 (following on from εἰ + perfect indicative), and similarly in §54.

Further points to note:

(i) οὐδ' ἄν is used to signify "not even if x happens" rather than "were to happen": cf. in §10, μηδ' ἄν in §67, and similarly κἄν (= καὶ ἄν), "even if", in §17, καὶ .. ἄν in §70.

(ii) Duplicated ἄντε functions like εἴτε ... εἴτε, "whether ... or", but with generalising force: see in §§16, 69.

C.3.a

Indefinite clauses in primary sequence, type "Whoever does this is automatically put to death" (remember that English often dispenses with the suffix "-ever"):

(a) Subjunctive + ἄν in conjunction with a part of the ordinary relative pronoun ὅς (§44); or of ὅστις (§54).

(b) ἐπειδάν (= ἐπειδή + ἄν) with aorist subjunctive, "whenever/ once (whenever that may be) *x* has", cf. in §§35, 69 (with perfect subjunctive εἰδῆτε in §65, "once you have come to realise"); with aorist then present in §50 ("whenever he has attacked and nobody is willing to take the field"). — ὅταν (= ὅτε + ἄν) with present subjunctive in §19 ("whenever = "when at some point in the future you want to").

C.3.b

ἕως ἄν in primary sequence with present subjunctive, "as long as": §§13, 69; with aorist subjunctive (and so πρὶν ἄν in §53), "until *x* has ...": §§10, 17.

C.4.a

Final or purpose clauses, type "He does/ did this in order to be noticed". Five cases, all introduced by ἵνα (no ἄν remember; negative μή), four of them in primary sequence (§§8, 20, 64, 71), one (§26) in historic (the so-called "vivid" use of the subjunctive, here specifying a circumstance *continuing into the present*).

C.4.b

Object clause with verb expressing a prospective fear, "be afraid that (μή) *x* may/ might happen": §§1/ 65; 54. — Object clause with δια-τηρεῖν, "watch to make sure that ... not (μή)": §20.

C.5

The "independent" uses of the subjunctive are represented by:

(i) Deliberative, type "what am I/ are we to do?" First person singular §§18, 46, in indirect clause §§4, 54; plural §70.

(ii) Exhortation in first person plural, "let us ...": §71 (twice). — Prohibition in (aorist) third person singular, §16, "let nobody (μηδείς) say".

(iii) Emphatic denial, οὐ μή + third person aorist: §75.

D. SYNTAX OF THE OPTATIVE

D.1

ἄν + optative in a hypothetical statement ("potential" optative), type "It would (could should etc.) be", in §16 "it could be", "it is perhaps". 10x in all.

D.2.a

The aforementioned brand of optative + ἄν in the *apodosis*, εἰ + optative in the *protasis*, in a condition of the type "If I were to do this, you would be angry". Examples in §§14, 18.

D.2.b

εἰ + optative to mark indefinite frequency in past time (ctr. under C.2(b)), §11 εἴ τις ... "if <ever> anyone", "whenever anybody"; so in §61.

D.3

Indefinite clauses in secondary sequence (ctr. under C.3.a). Examples in §§23 (introduced by ὅ τι, "whatever"), 45 (introduced by οὕς, "whomsoever").

D.4

Third person aorist to express a wish, "may x happen", "I hope that x happens":
§76; with negative μή, §65.

NOTES

Before looking at each portion of the text:
(i) Read carefully through the summary of the argument.
(ii) Study the Vocabulary. It lists a number of words which are well worth committing to memory; those of lesser importance are dealt with in the running commentary. *Not* included are the very commonest words: any still unfamiliar to you as you work through the text should be looked up (try Liddell and Scott's *Intermediate Greek Lexicon*), jotted down and memorised at the earliest opportunity.

"*MS*" refers to the introductory notes on Morphology and Syntax.

It has generally been inferred from certain peculiarities in the transmission of this speech that a number of passages, varying in length from a few words to several lines, are derived from a slightly expanded version which goes back to Demosthenes himself (cf. in §§2, 6, 7, 20, 26, 32, 37 (x2), 39, 41, 44, 46, 58, 65, 71). It is far more likely, as W. Bühler* has argued, that nearly all of them are interpolated: for the purposes of this edition a translation (that of A.W. Pickard-Cambridge) of these passages, bracketed { }, will be given as they occur.

* See "Suggestions for further reading" below.

***

Synopsis
§§1-5 Philip must be stopped: it spite of all it is not too late.
§§8-20 His "peace" is a sham — he will strike without warning when he so chooses; in fact, he has flagrantly violated the terms of the peace by his acts of aggression and intrigues against various Greek states. Though the security of the Chersonese and Byzantium is a priority, we must consider as a matter of urgency how to deal with the danger facing the Greek world in its entirety.
§§21-35 Philip has been allowed to grow immensely strong by a disunited Greece. He has wiped out city after city and is active everywhere; no Greek himself, he has even presided over the Pythian Games! Whatever outrage he commits, the Greeks are busy mistrusting one another rather than him.
§§36-46 The spirit that saw off the Persians is no longer with us, and corruption, dealt with severely hitherto, is prevalent.

§§47-52 Philip's improved methods of warfare have made it impossible for Athens to combat him single-handed; operations must be conducted against him away from our home-base.

§§53-75 Given what happened at Olynthus and elsewhere his partisans here in Athens must be silenced. A resolution must be passed to ensure that liberty is preserved: Athens must take the initiative in calling upon all states to unite in order to deal effectively with Philip.

§§1-5

Early summer 341 BC. [1] Although many speeches have been delivered on Philip's illegal acts ever since the Peace, and although it is agreed that he must be stopped, our position could not possibly be made worse than it is at present. [2] This is mainly because of those self-seeking or malicious speakers who prefer gratifying you to giving you the best advice. [3] You must not be angry if, in speaking the truth, I avail myself of that freedom of speech which is the right of all those who live in Athens, but which you have banished from the political arena. [4] You allow yourselves to be flattered while your vital interests are endangered. If you will listen to one who will give you sound advice without flattery, I am ready to speak. Much has been sacrificed; but, if you are willing to do your duty, the position may be retrieved. [5] The best hope for the future lies in the fact that this sorry state of affairs has come about while you have been entirely neglecting your duty. Philip has conquered your inertia and negligence, but has not conquered your country: so far from having been defeated yourselves, you have not even stirred.

Vocabulary
Nouns

ἀμέλεια, ἡ	lack of care, negligence
ἐκκλησία, ἡ	assembly (-meeting)
ἐξουσία, ἡ	authority, permission, licence, freedom of action
παρρησία, ἡ	outspokenness, freedom of speech
πρόνοια, ἡ	forethought, provident concern
ῥᾳθυμία, ἡ	indifference, sluggishness, inertia
δίκη, ἡ	penalty: δίκην διδόναι pay a penalty, be chastised; δίκην λαμβάνειν exact a penalty (παρά + gen., from)
εἰρήνη, ἡ	peace
οἰκέτης, ὁ	household servant, menial
ξένος, ὁ	foreigner (opp. πολίτης)

αἴτιον, τό	reason, cause; adj. αἴτιος responsible (for, gen.)
ὕβρις, ἡ	outrageous behaviour
ἔνιοι -αι -α	as substantive, some
Adjectives	
ἕτοιμος	ready, prepared (to, infin.)
συνήθης	familiar, customary
Verbs	
δια-βάλλειν	misrepresent, slander
ἐξ-ελαύνειν	drive out, expel, banish
ἐξ-ετάζειν	subject [a question] to close examination or scrutiny
κινδυνεύειν	run a risk
προσ-ήκειν	(as impersonal) be appropriate, proper
συμ-βαίνειν	(as impersonal) turn out, happen
συμ-βουλεύειν	give advice, counsel
συμ-φέρειν	(as impersonal) be advantageous, in one's interest
παύεσθαι	(with gen.) desist from
χαρίζεσθαι	seek to win favour, ingratiate oneself
αἰτιᾶσθαι	accuse, censure
ἡττᾶσθαι	be worsted, defeated
κρατεῖν	(with gen.) become master of, prevail over
χειροτονεῖν	vote for (by a show of hands), carry (a motion)
ἡγεῖσθαι	think, suppose
προ-αιρεῖσθαι	prefer, choose deliberately/ as a matter of policy (to)
ἀξιοῦν	(with acc./ infin.) think it appropriate that, demand/ insist that
μετα-διδόναι	grant one (dat.) a share in (gen.), allow one to participate in
Adverbs	
ἴσως	perhaps, maybe
ὀρθῶς	properly, correctly
φαύλως	in a poor/ sorry state
εἶτα	then, next; hence, consequently
παντάπασι(ν)	altogether, completely
πάνυ	very

Preposition

χωρίς   (with gen.) apart from, without

Aids to comprehension

§1

πολλῶν ... φησάντων γ᾽ ἄν: One genitive absolute, stating a fact, is followed up at
once with another, cast in hypothetical form, with change of subject; πολλῶν is
balanced by πάντων. Translate as concessive clauses, "although ..."

λόγων γιγνομένων: γίγνεσθαι ("be produced") serves as passive of the middle
ποιεῖσθαι, with λόγους "make, deliver speeches".

ὀλίγου δεῖν: A specimen of the so-called "absolute infinitive" (like the familiar ὡς
(ἔπος) εἰπεῖν [cf. in §47]), δεῖν *with genitive* bearing the sense "need, require":
"so as to need little" = "virtually, all but"; closely with καθ᾽ ἑκάστην.

ὧν ... ἀδικεῖ: A case of "relative attraction", the equivalent of τούτων ἃ ὑμᾶς
ἀδικεῖ (double accusative, present tense of effects extending to the time of
speaking), "... the criminal measures Philip, ever since (ἀφ᾽ οὗ, literally "from
which point") he concluded ..., has been taking and persists in taking against
you".

τὴν εἰρήνην: The so-called Peace of Philocrates, 346 BC.

τοὺς ἄλλους: "the others" = "everybody else" in Greece, "Athens and the rest of
Greece".

οἶδ(α) [cf. *MS* A.2.a] ὅτι is parenthetic (cf. δῆλον ὅτι ~ δηλονότι), "I know that
<x is/ would be the case>", a stereotyped way of saying "of this I'm sure".

φησάντων γ᾽ ἄν: ἔφησα is the aorist (though imperfect ἔφην regularly has an
aoristic force) of φάναι: "would certainly say".

εἰ καὶ .. τοῦτο: A cutting aside: "even if they do not (actually) do this (particular
thing, specified in the call for "words *plus* actions", καὶ λέγειν δεῖν καὶ
πράττειν ...)" means "even if they do not act on what they say".

... πράττειν ὅπως ...: "that both words and actions must be directed towards
ensuring that he is going to ...", ὅπως with future as often expressing the object
of endeavour: cf. in §§2, 29, 51, 56, 59, 61, 63, 69, 75.

εἰς τοῦθ᾽ ... ὁρῶ: Now the principal clause, though it is of relatively short duration.

ὑπηγμένα ... προειμένα: On these perfects see *MS* A.4.b: "I observe that
[participles with verb of perception] all your interests have been insidiously
undermined, and sacrificed, to this point/ to the point that ..." ὑπ-ηγμένα
literally "gradually brought (to a point) by underhand methods", the preverb
combining the notions of "little by little" and "covertly"; προ-ειμέν(α) from
προ-ιέναι (~ προ-ίημι), "let go, dismiss, throw away, surrender".

δέδοικα ... ᾖ: δέδοικα perfect: *MS* A.3.a; on the use of the subjunctive see *MS*
C.4.b. The mode of expression, "I fear that it <may be> a slanderous/ offensive
thing to say, but that it may be (turn out to be) true", betrays the Greek love of

20

antithesis. We might prefer to say "It may be ... to say, but I am afraid that it could prove true".

καὶ (... καί): Not εἰ καί as above, but "both (... and)".

οἱ παρ-ιόντες: "those who step forward <to address you>", "speakers in the ecclesia". In contemporary Attic prose, with very few exceptions, ἰών ἰοῦσα ἰόν serves as present participle of ἔρχομαι (cf. παρ-ιόντα in §17, ἐπ-ιόντα in §22, προσ-ιόντος in §61; so subjunctive ἐξ-ίῃ §50, and also imperfect προσ-ῇεσαν §61).

ὑμεῖς: "you", their audience: supply ἐβούλεσθε.

ἐξ ὧν ... ἕξειν: (to put forward ... to pass) "<resolutions/ proposals> as a result of which your affairs were to be in the sorriest state possible", "... your position was bound to be the most desperate imaginable".

ὡς with superlative adverb, literally "as ... as possible"; ἔμελλε (this verb often expresses certainty, inevitability) singular: neuter plural subject (cf. ἐστίν and ἀφῖκται in §2, ἔχει and προεῖται in §4, ἔχει and διέκειτο in §5); ἕξειν: ἔχειν with adverb means "be".

ἄν: The postpositive is slotted into second position in the sense-unit; it belongs with δύνασθαι, "that they could be rendered worse than <they are> at the present time".

χεῖρον: χείρων -ονος serves as a comparative of κακός (cf. the superlative χείριστον in §5).

δια-τεθῆναι: Aorist passive infinitive of δια-τιθέναι, with adverb "put in a certain condition, dispose in a certain way ", cf. on διάκεισθε in §4.

§2

οὐ ... δύ(ο): "not by a margin of one thing, or of two things either", i.e. "not as a result of a single cause, or two causes only", "not from any one or two causes".

ἀφ-ῖκται: Perfect, see MS A.4.b.

ἄν-περ = ἐάν-περ, with subjunctive: see MS C.2; "if in fact/ only".

τὰ βέλτιστα λέγειν: Cf. on §56.

ἐν οἷς is picked up by ταῦτα: "in spheres in which they personally (αὐτοί, "themselves") enjoy high esteem/ popularity and power/ influence — it is here that they seek to maintain the status quo, and so ...". With εὐδοκιμοῦσιν cf. δοκεῖν, "be reputed", δόξα, "reputation, repute"; φυλάττοντες is a present participle expressing endeavour/ effort.

τῶν μελλόντων: Neuter plural participle (cf. in §5), = "the future".

{οὐκοῦν ... ἔχειν "and therefore think that you also should take none (i.e. no thought for the future)".}

τοὺς ... ὄντας (cf. in §56): "those in charge of (state) administration", those actively engaged in <the necessary> policy-making.

οὐδὲν ἄλλο ... λήψεται: Cf. in §1 above: "do nothing other than <ensure> how ...", i.e. "concentrate all their efforts on ensuring that ... will ..."

αὐτὴ παρ' αὑτῆς: As often, a part of αὐτός, "-self", reinforces the reflexive αὑτ-: "will inflict punishment on herself", that is on her very own citizen-body.

περὶ τοῦτ' ἔσται: "will be engaged around (= in) this particular thing", hence "will be fully occupied in doing so", distracted and so blind to the threat from outside.

§3

πολιτεῖαι: "ways of conducting affairs of state", "political methods".

ἄν: i.e. ἐάν, with subjunctive: *MS* C.2.

τι τῶν ἀληθῶν: "some degree of (the) true things": "if I am outspoken enough to spell out some <unpalatable> truths".

ὡδί: "this way", "like this", the so-called "deictic" (δεικνύναι, "to point out") form of ὧδε, cf. οὑτωσί beside οὕτως, and see in §§12, 22, 23, 36, 44, 72.

ἐπὶ .. τῶν ἄλλων: "in all other spheres".

μετα-δεδώκατε: Perfect: cf. *MS* A.3.a.

πλείονος: Irregular comparative of πολύς.

τοῦ συμβουλεύειν: Articular infinitive (*MS* B), "the business/ process of giving advice" in deliberative meetings of the Assembly: there is no freedom of speech where it really matters, in the political arena.

ἐξ-εληλάκατε: On the perfect see *MS* A.3.a.

§4

συμ-βέβηκεν perfect: *MS* A.3.a; see introductory Vocabulary: the verb takes dative + infinitive, literally "to you that <you> ..."

τρυφᾶν: "be spoilt, pampered, petted, overindulged", κολακεύεσθαι: "be flattered" (cf. ἡ κολακεία below).

πάντα ... ἀκούουσιν: "listening to all things with a view to pleasure", i.e. "listening as you do only to what affords you pleasure/ gratification".

ἐν ... γιγνομένοις: "in the (actual) conduct of affairs and in day-to-day [*present participle*] events".

περὶ τῶν ἐσχάτων ...: "run risks for the most extreme things", i.e. "run the gravest risks".

καὶ νῦν: "even now", after all that has happened.

οὕτω διάκεισθε: The verb in conjunction with an adverb means (cf. on διατεθῆναι in §1, and see *MS* A.2.b) "be disposed in a certain way", "have such and such an attitude", "be in a certain state or condition" (cf. in §§5, 28, 61 below).

οὐκ ... λέγω: "I do not know what I can say" (on the subjunctive cf. *MS* C.5.(i)).

εἰ ... ἐθελήσετ(ε): εἰ with future (rather than ἐάν with subjunctive) is in keeping with the tone of urgency: "if you will consent".

ἕτοιμος: Supply "I am".

καὶ γὰρ εἰ: καί with εἰ, "even if it is the case that ..."

φαύλως ... ἔχει: Cf. in §1.

προεῖται: See on προειμένα in §1.

ἔστιν (note accent) for ἔξεστιν.

ἐάν clause: *MS* C.2.

τὰ δέοντα [~ δεῖν]: "the necessary things", "one's duty" (so again in §5).

ἐπ-αν-ορθώσασθαι: ἐπ-αν-ορθοῦσθαι, "put in an upright position [~ adj. ὀρθός] once more [ἀνα- = "back again"]", hence "set straight/ right again, remedy".

§5

χείριστον: Cf. on χεῖρον in §1.

τοῖς παρ-εληλυθόσι: Perfect participle of παρ-ιέναι/ παρ-έρχομαι (*MS* A.3.a), neuter plural τὰ παρ-εληλυθότα = "past events", "the past", opp. τὰ μέλλοντα (cf. in §2).

ὑπ-άρχει: ὑπ-άρχειν can mean "be there", "be available": so here "is the best basis/ foundation for ..."

οὔτε ... ὑμῶν: Genitive absolute, balanced in the next clause by πάνθ' ... πραττόντων (supply ὑμῶν).

οὔτε μικρὸν οὔτε μέγ' οὐδέν: "no aspect, either [duplication of negatives] small or great" is a way of saying "no aspect whatsoever".

ἐπεί τοι: "because, mark my words".

οὕτω διέκειτο: Cf. on διάκεισθε in §4.

οὐδ' .. ἐλπὶς .. γενέσθαι: Note aorist rather than future infinitive; "not even a hope of their becoming ..."

ἄν with imperfect, "would be".

βελτίω: Neuter plural comparative (cf. superlative βέλτιστον above) of ἀγαθός, alternative form βελτίονα.

νῦν δέ: As often "but as things stand", "but as it is".

τῆς ῥᾳθυμίας τῆς ὑμετέρας ...: Prominently placed: "it is your [cf. emphatic ὑμεῖς shortly] ... that ..."

κεκράτηκε perfect: *MS* A.3.a.

τῆς πόλεως δ': δέ commonly follows the sequence article-substantive.

ἀλλ' οὐδὲ κεκίνησθε: Sarcastic: "on the contrary, you have not so much as [been set in motion/ set yourselves in motion ~] stirred yourselves [~ mobilised]!". On the perfect see *MS* A.4.a.

{§§6-7

εἰ μὲν οὖν ... δεῖ ...]: [§6] "Now if it was admitted by us all that Philip was at war with Athens, and was transgressing the Peace, a speaker would have to do nothing but to advise you as to the safest and easiest method of resistance to him. But since there are some who are in so extraordinary a frame of mind that, though he is capturing cities, though many of your possessions are in his hands, and though he is committing aggressions against all men, they still tolerate certain speakers, who constantly assert at your meetings that it is some of *us* who are provoking the war, it is necessary to be on our guard and come to a right understanding on the matter. [§7] For there is a danger lest any one who proposes or advises resistance should find himself accused of having brought about the war. Well, I say this first of all, and lay it down as a principle, that if it is open to us to deliberate whether we should remain at peace or should go to war ..."}

§§8-9

[8] If peace depends on ourselves, we should maintain it; but if another party offers the pretence of peace and resorts to acts of war, we must defend ourselves. [9] The peace envisaged by Philip is a wholly one-sided affair: it is to procure such a peace that he is spending all this money.

Vocabulary
Adjective

λοιπός	left over, remaining
Verbs	
ἀν-αλίσκειν	spend (money)
ὑπο-λαμβάνειν	suppose, understand (with acc., *x* <to be> so-and-so)
φάσκειν	assert, profess, allege
ἀμύνεσθαι	defend oneself
δια-φέρεσθαι	have a difference of opinion, quarrel [with, dat.]
μαίνεσθαι	be mad, out of one's mind
ὠνεῖσθαι	buy, purchase
Adverb	
ἐντεῦθεν	hence, from/with this point
Conjunction	
πλήν	except

Aids to comprehension

§8

εἰρήνην ἄγειν: "be at/ maintain peace".

ἐφ' ἡμῖν ...: "this decision is in our power/ rests with us".

ἵν' .. ἄρξωμαι: Final clause, MS C.4.a.

γράφειν in the technical sense of "put forward a motion", "formally propose measures" <to that effect>, cf. in §§70, 76.

πράττειν: "act <accordingly: on the basis of his proposals, instead of just talking>".

φενακίζειν: "cheat, trick, prevaricate", by not having the slightest intention of taking action.

δύναμιν: "power", here in the sense "(armed) force, forces".

αὐτόν: Note the aspiration: reflexive.

τοὔνομα ...: Crasis, τὸ ὄνομα; emphatic, balanced by τοῖς δ' ἔργοις ... at the head of the next clause, "puts forward/ holds out to you [as a screen: he shelters behind it] the *name* <and only the name> of peace, while the *acts* to which he himself resorts are acts of war" (χρῆται from χρῆσθαι, "use, employ").

τί ...: Supply "is".

εἰ βούλεσθε comes late in the clause, so highlighting the cutting φάσκειν ..., "*to profess* that you are ...": if you want, like Philip, to maintain a *nominal* peace, while *actually* waging war, fine.

§9

ταύτην rather than a neuter, gender assimilated to the ensuing predicate.

ἐξ ἧς: "<a peace> on the basis of which".

τἄλλα: τὰ ἄλλα.

ἔπειτ' ("then", "in the second place") as commonly lacks a δέ to answer the πρῶτον μέν.

ἐκείνῳ ... λέγει i.e. "the peace he talks about is one observed towards him by you ..."

τῶν ... πάντων: Genitive of price, "with all the money that is [continually: present participle] being spent by him".

αὐτὸς ... is heralded by τοῦτο ...: "<viz.> that he himself should ..."

πολεμεῖν ... πολεμεῖσθαι: Note the chiasmus: *abba*.

§§10-14

[10-12] It is Philip's policy to pretend to be at peace until the last possible moment. Consider the cases of Olynthus, Phocis, Pherae and Oreus. [13-14] Since he has practised deception on harmless foes he will never actually declare war on

you; *and he will never make it impossible for his partisans to assure you that* he *is not making war against you.*

Vocabulary
Nouns

εὔνοια, ἡ	goodwill, benevolence; κατ᾽ εὔνοιαν, in a spirit of goodwill
καιρός, ὁ	critical time
πρέσβεις, οἱ	ambassadors

Adjectives

ἀληθινός	true, genuine
τελευταῖος	last, final; adv. τὰ τελευταῖα [cf. e.g. τὰ πρῶτα] lastly
εὐήθης	simple-minded, silly, naive

Verbs

ἀπ-έχειν	(intransitive, with gen.) be away, distant from
βαδίζειν	go/ come (on foot), march, advance
κατα-λαμβάνειν	seize, occupy
προ-λέγειν	say in advance, forewarn, caution
βιάζεσθαι	employ force, coercion
πορεύεσθαι	go, march
τεκμαίρεσθαι	(with dat.) base a judgement on, judge by
ἐξ-απατᾶν	deceive
ἀγανακτεῖν	be indignant, take it hard
ἐγ-καλεῖν	(with dat.) bring a charge against
ἐπι-σκοπεῖν	~ future -σκέψεσθαι visit (as one might a sick patient)
ἀπο-λογεῖσθαι	speak in one's own or another's support or defence (against a formal accusation)

Adverb

πρώην	just lately

Preposition

μέχρι	(with gen.) up to (a point in time), till

Particle

μήν	καὶ μήν and what is more, a further point

26

Aids to comprehension

§10

εἰ with future is here used as an equivalent of μέλλειν + infinitive, "if we are going/ mean to wait"; περιμενοῦμεν: note the form of this future.

ἕως ἂν .. ὁμολογήσῃ: "until such time as he admits to being at war with us"; on ἕως ἄν with aorist subjunctive cf. *MS* C.3.b.

ἄν i.e. ἐάν, with subjunctive: *MS* C.2.

ἐρεῖ: Future of λέγειν.

εἴ-περ: "if really, if in fact", here a confident "if, as the facts suggest", "if, as must be the case".

οἷς i.e. τούτοις ἃ ...

τοὺς ἄλλους: Cf. on τοὺς ἄλλους in §1.

πεποίηκε perfect: *MS* A.3.a.

§11

τοῦτο μὲν γάρ is answered in due course by τοῦτο δ᾽, literally "in respect of this", i.e. "on the one hand ..., on the other", "first ..., secondly". "Take the case of Olynthians/ Olynthus: ...; then there is his treatment of Phocians/ Phocis:".

Ὀλυνθίοις ... : The inhabitants of Olynthus in Chalcidice. The occasion referred to is Philip's declaration of war in 349 BC.

τετταράκοντ᾽ ... στάδια: Accusative of extent, "by/ at a distance of".

δεῖ: The present reflects the tense of the original statement (cf. νοσοῦσι καὶ στασιάζουσιν in §12, and the future infinitive λυσιτελήσειν shortly).

δυοῖν θάτερον: δυοῖν is genitive of the dual δύο, θάτερον = τὸ ἕτερον (note the anomalous contraction), an accusative of respect, "with regard to (the) one of two things/ alternatives", effectively functioning as an adverbial phrase heralding ἤ/ ἤ; we might render "it was necessary to make a choice: either they should ..., or, alternatively, he himself <should> ..."

ἤ ...: Supply μὴ οἰκεῖν.

πάντα τὸν ἄλλον χρόνον: Accusative of duration, τὸν ἄλλον bearing the sense "the rest of/ the whole <before that>".

εἴ τις ...: The optative is one of indefinite frequency (*MS* D.2.b), "if <ever>/ whenever anybody ..."; αἰτιάσαιτο here with two accusatives.

ἀγανακτῶν καὶ .. πέμπων: Translate by means of a concessive clause, "though he ..."

τοὺς ἀπολογησομένους: Future participle (cf. ἐπισκεψομένους in §12) expressing purpose; the definite article, specifying a particular body of individuals, can be represented by something like "sending his people as ambassadors to ..."

εἰς Φωκέας ὡς πρὸς συμμάχους: "into (the midst of) Phocians as though to allies", i.e. "into Phocis, ostensibly to deal with an allied power". This was in 346 BC. Philip insisted that Phocis be excluded from any alliance with Athens.

Later, in *On the Crown,* §§35-36 (transl. Usher), Demosthenes exclaimed against an implacable opponent: "What, then, were the words that Aeschines uttered at that time, and which caused everything to be ruined? He said we should not be alarmed by Philip's advance past Thermopylae ... 'It is in the interest of Philip, the Phocians and you, all alike, to be rid of the thick-skinned oppressiveness of the Thebans'. Some were happy to listen to these words of his because of the underlying hatred towards the Thebans at that time. What happened immediately after that, not some time later? The Phocians were ruined, their cities razed to the ground..."

ἐπορεύετο: With this and the succeeding imperfects the speaker adopts the perspective of one who witnessed these events unfolding.

παρ-ηκολούθουν: ἀκολουθεῖν with dative = "accompany", παρ- with dative = "by one's side": "were in close attendance on him".

παρ' ἡμῖν: "amongst us" here in Athens.

ἤριζον: ~ ἐρίζειν (ἔρις "strife, quarrel, dispute", cf. in §14) "contend vigorously", "maintain stoutly".

Θηβαίοις οὐ λυσιτελήσειν: "would not profit Thebans", i.e. would be anything but advantageous to Thebes.

πάροδον: "passing by" ~ "way past" ~ "mountain-pass", here of Philip's "passage through the pass <of Thermopylae>".

§12

καὶ μὴν καί introduces yet another example of Philip's aggressive behaviour: "and yes, there is the case of Pherae as well:". In 344 Philip took Pherae (for the third time) and installed a Macedonian garrison on its acropolis.

ἔχει καταλαβών: "has seized it and <still> occupies it".

τοῖς ... τουτοισί: "these miserable wretches the people of Oreus", the suffix -ί (literally "here", cf. on ὡδί in §3) suggesting that the fate that befell them is recent enough to prompt a vivid recollection. On these inhabitants of Euboea cf. in §§59-62.

πεπομφέναι: Perfect infinitive, *MS* A.3.a.

αὐτούς anticipates the subject of the ὡς clause, "them ... that they"; this can be reflected by translating "received a report about them to the effect that ..."

νοσοῦσι καὶ στασιάζουσιν: "were sick [cf. in §§39, 50] and were engaged in stasis", i.e. "were suffering from the malady of factional strife".

συμμάχων ... παρεῖναι: The genitives signify "<the mark, duty, function> of" ... to be at hand.

§13

εἶτ(α): Inferentially, "so".

οἵ is picked up by τούτους μὲν ..., "do you consider that in the case of people who could have done him no harm [had he declared war on them openly], but who (though they) in an effort to avoid being harmed <themselves> might conceivably have taken precautions, he chose ... *these*, whereas *in your case* he would ...?"

μὴ παθεῖν δ': This particle regularly comes after μή (or οὐ) + associated word.

ἐκ προρρήσεως: (ῥῆσις, "speech", "utterance") "on the basis of a prior statement", i.e. "by a formal declaration in advance".

καὶ ταῦθ': καὶ ταῦτα is a common way of saying "and that too".

ἕως ἂν ...: "as long as [*MS* C.3.b] you are willing(ly) deceived", i.e. "all the time that you are willing to have the wool pulled over your eyes".

§14

οὐκ ἔστι ταῦτα: Neuter plural subject, singular verb; ἔστι = ἔξεστι: "out of the question!"

ἀβελτερώτατος: ἀβέλτερος = "silly, simple-minded, fatuous".

τῶν ἀδικουμένων ... αἰτιωμένων: Genitives absolute; τῶν ἀδικουμένων is prominently placed: "you — the very victims of his criminal acts —".

μηδέν rather than οὐδέν because the participle ("so long as you ...") has quasi-conditional force.

ὑμῶν αὐτῶν: Second person reflexive, people "from among your own citizen-body".

ἐκεῖνος: Emphatic: *"he"* of all people.

φιλονικίαν: Whether spelled -νικίαν or (as in the manuscripts) -νεικίαν, the word is certainly associated here with νεῖκος (τό, a synonym of ἔρις), "love of strife", rather than νίκη: "dissolve/ resolve the wrangling ... and the argumentativeness to which you are addicted".

ἐφ' αὑτόν: With τρέπεσθαι.

προ-είποι: Sarcastic: "invite you publicly" to ...

τῶν ... ἀφ-έλοιτο: "take away from those who receive wages [μισθός, ὁ] from his own hand (are in his own pay) the arguments ..."

ἀνα-βάλλουσιν: "put off", "make you defer action".

ἐκεῖνος γ': *"he* at any rate" (whatever others may have in mind).

§§15-20

[15-17] Philip is proved by his naked acts of aggression and his intrigues in the Chersonese, Euboea, Thrace and elsewhere to have broken the terms of the Peace; preparations for attack are as much acts of war as the attack itself. [18-20] Success for him will have grave consequences, and you must act at once. The

Chersonese and Byzantium must be safeguarded, but you should now be making the peril of the whole of Greece the subject of your deliberations.

Vocabulary
Noun

λογισμός, ὁ	reasoning, reasoned argument, conclusion

Adjective

κύριος	(with gen.) in control of, exercising authority over

Verbs

ἐπ-αμύνειν	(with dat.) render assistance to
μετ-έχειν	(with gen.) share in, share
παρα-βαίνειν	transgress, offend against
τοξεύειν	use a bow, shoot an arrow
ὑγιαίνειν	be healthy, of sound mind
ἅπτεσθαι	(with gen.) take hold of; of an aggressor, fasten on, lay hands on, attempt to seize
λογίζεσθαι	reckon, reason
ἀν-αιρεῖν	do away with, wipe out, destroy
βοηθεῖν	render active (military) assistance
ληρεῖν	talk nonsense
σωφρονεῖν	be wise, prudent
καθ-ιστάναι	station, post

Adverbs

ἄρτι	lately, just
αὖθις	hereafter, in future
ἡνίκα	when

Preposition

πρός	(with gen.) in the name of

Particles

δήπου	surely
καίτοι	(and) yet

Aids to comprehension
§15
ὦ πρὸς τοῦ Διός: An exasperated "in heaven's name".

ὅστις εὖ φρονῶν: "anyone in his right mind who ...", εὖ φρονεῖν = "be sane", "be right in the head".

ἐκ: "on the basis of".

ὀνομάτων are here "words" as opposed to actions.

τὸν ... σκέψαιτ᾽ ἄν: "would consider the person who was ... or who was ...", i.e. "would consider the issue of whether a person was ... or was ..."

τοίνυν reactivates the account of Philip's acts of aggression: "now", "well then". — In fact, these operations were carried out after peace had been sworn by the Athenians, but *before* the Athenian envoys had administered the oaths to Philip. The Thracian king Cersebleptes was in any case excluded from the terms of the Peace.

ἐξ ἀρχῆς ... ἐλάμβανε: The prepositional phrase is defined more closely by the succeeding genitives absolute: "<going into action> right from the start, when ..., proceeded to take ..."

γεγονυίας: Perfect (active version) of γίγνεσθαι (*MS* A.3.a), the verb serving here as passive of (τὴν εἰρήνην) ποιεῖσθαι (cf. in §1 init.).

Διοπείθους: Athenian cleruchs [see *Oxford Classical Dictionary*, ed.3, pp.347-8] were sent to the Chersonese under his leadership in the summer of 343.

τῶν ὄντων ... νῦν: "who are now" (at the time of speaking).

ἀπ-εσταλμένων: Perfect participle passive (*MS* A.4.b) of ἀπο-στέλλειν, "dispatch".

Σέρριον ...: Serrium: a headland on the southern coast of Thrace ("Serreian τεῖχος" its coastal fort, Athenian-manned, one of a number of defensive works hurriedly established along the Propontid and Aegean coasts), west of the Hebrus, near the mouth of which Doriscus lay. "Holy Mountain" on the Propontis was the royal stronghold of Cersebleptes, captured by Philip on April 21.

ἐκ anticipates the preverb ἐξ-; we would say "those *in* the fort ... he expelled".

στρατηγός: This was Chares.

κατέστησεν: Translate with a pluperfect.

§16

ταῦτα ... ἐποίει; "in making these moves what was he (effectively) doing?"

ὠμωμόκει: Pluperfect of ὀμνύναι (*MS* A.5), with accusative: "<I put this question> because it was *peace* he had sworn". (The unanswered μέν carries the implication "whereas his actions were those of a *belligerent*").

μηδεὶς εἴπῃ: Third person singular aorist subjunctive in a prohibition (*MS* C.5.(ii)): "don't let anybody say". The orator Aeschines [cf. in §11] was later to accuse Demosthenes of "discovering" the places he mentions here.

τί δὲ ταῦτ᾽ ἐστίν; Singular verb: neuter plural subject (cf. ἔχει below in the wake of a pair of neuter singular substantives): "But what of it?/ So what?" δέ in such expressions is, like our "but" and "and", indicative of impatience, exasperation, indignation.

τί ... μέλει ...; Impersonal μέλει: μέλει μοι (cf. in §45) τούτου, "there is a concern to me about this", "I am concerned about this"; so here "how do these matters concern Athens?"

εἰ ... οὗτος: "whether they <were> trivial, or <whether> ..., this could be (is perhaps: *MS* D.1) another matter/ a different question" (not pertinent to the subject under discussion). οὗτος: gender assimilated to the preceding substantive, cf. on ταύτην in §9.

τὸ δ᾽ εὐσεβὲς ...: "But <and this *is* relevant> observance of religious principles, and fair-dealing <towards both gods and one's fellow-men> [to which one is obliged to adhere by virtue of having sworn an oath] ... have the same <binding> force [impose the same obligation to stick to one's word in either of the two circumstances specified in the intervening clause ἄν τ᾽ ἐπὶ μικροῦ ...]".

ἄν τ᾽ ... ἄν τ᾽ with subjunctive (*MS* C.2(ii)) = ἐάντε ... ἐάντε, the generalising form of εἴτε ... εἴτε, "whether ... or".

ἐπὶ μικροῦ ...: "in (the case of) a trivial matter, or in a serious matter"; μείζονος is an instance of the "contrasting" comparative (cf. in §69), not "greater" but "great, rather <than the opposite, just specified>".

φέρε like ἄγε (used even in an address to a plurality) "come".

δή with an imperative = "now", "then".

εἰς Χερρόνησον ...: Early in 341 Philip had sent troops in support of Cardia, a city on the west side of the Thracian Chersonese which emphatically denied the claim of Athens to supremacy over her, and claimed independence. Nothing is known of any formal recognition of Athens' claim to the Chersonese by Persia and the Greeks.

βασιλεύς without the article is the usual way of referring to the king of Persia.

ἐγνώκασιν: Perfect of γιγνώσκειν (*MS* A.3.b), "have judged, acknowledged".

ξένους: Here "mercenaries".

ἐπι-στέλλει ταῦτα: "writes to you [~ ἐπιστολή, "letter", "missive"] to this effect".

§17

φησί: "he *says*" [but what is he actually *doing*?].

τοσούτου δέω ... ὁμολογεῖν: "I need so much [cf. on ὀλίγου δεῖν in §1] to admit that he" = "So far am I from admitting ..."

Μεγάρων: The reference is to an unsuccessful coup staged in 343 with the aid of troops supplied by Philip.

κἄν = καὶ ἐν.

τυραννίδα: τυραννίδας plural according to the quotation in the rhetorician Libanius (4 AD); τυραννίδα all MSS. It is true that more than one τύραννος was in question (cf. in §§57-62), but the singular might be used sweepingly, "a tyrannical mode of government": compare §27 init.

κατα-σκευάζοντα: "constructing, establishing, setting up", with a suggestion of devious behaviour.

ἐπὶ Θρᾴκην παριόντα: On -ιόντα cf. in §1; "advancing to attack". A campaign against Thrace had been initiated in 342, and was carried on until mid-340.

τὰν [τὰ ἐν] ... σκευωρούμενον: "cooking up the things in ...", i.e. "pursuing his Peloponnesian intrigues". Demosthenes is thinking of Philip's overtures to those who had no time for Lacedaemonians (notably Argives, Messenians, Arcadians), as well as of factions within the various cities.

μετὰ τῆς δυναμέως: Cf. on δύναμιν in §8; "with the help of/ by bringing into play his armed forces".

λύειν: "loosen, dissolve", hence "break, contravene, violate".

εἰ μὴ ... φήσετε: "— unless you are going/ are prepared to say".

τοὺς ... ἐφ-ιστάντας: "people who set up siege-engines for the purposes of launching an attack".

ἕως ἄν with aorist subjunctive, "until" (MS C.3.b).

ἤδη: "by this time", i.e. actually reach the point where they ...

(προσ)αγάγωσιν: Subjunctive of ἄγειν's aorist ἀγαγεῖν, tense ἤγαγον: "plant them against the walls".

ὁ ... κατασκευαζόμενος: "he who by means of which I might be captured, these means ...", i.e. "an individual who adopts the measures and contrives the means to secure my capture — he ..." A generalisation taking the speaker's own reaction to threatening behaviour of this kind as typical.

κἂν ... i.e. καὶ ἐάν, with subjunctive (MS C.2), "even if he isn't yet at the stage of discharging a missile or ..."

§18

τίσιν ... γένοιτο; "by reason of what things would you ...if anything were to happen?" That is to say, "in what circumstances would you be exposed to danger in the event of something <untoward> [such as a military setback] happening?"

τῷ ...: A series of three articular infinitives (MS B), the datives corresponding to τίσιν (see above), i.e. "in the ... "

τῷ ... ἀλλοτριωθῆναι (~ adj. ἀλλότριος "belonging to someone else", cf. in §73): "the - the Hellespont [accusative because of change of subject: so with the other two in the series] - to be put/ fall into other hands", "the alienation of the H." For the reference to the Hellespont cf. on §27.

τἀκείνου [τὰ ἐκείνου] φρονῆσαι: "coming to [aorist] think the things pertaining to" is an idiomatic way of saying "coming to sympathise with his cause", "coming over to his side".

εἶτα inferentially, "then", "so".

φῶ: Deliberative subjunctive (aorist of φάναι) , "am I to say?", "can I say?": *MS* C.5(i).

§19

πολλοῦ γε καὶ δεῖ (cf. on ὀλίγου δεῖν in §1): "there is in fact need of much indeed": "Why, far from it! (ἀλλ᾽) On the contrary ..."
ἀφ᾽: "from which day" is a condensed way of saying "from the day <on which>".
ἀνεῖλε Φωκέας: Cf. on §11.
ὁρίζομαι: "mark out (as) a boundary", "define", "determine", here with accusative and infinitive: "*I* reckon that his being at war with you dates from ..."
ὑμᾶς δ᾽: The pronoun is prominently placed: "as for the action that you should take —"
ἐάν with subjunctive: *MS* C.2.
ἤδη: Here in the sense "right now", "instantly".
ἐάσητε: ἐᾶν commonly means "leave alone, let be": "let the occasion go by, let things slip". This lively word is supplanted in most MSS by ἀναβάλλησθε, "put things off".
ὅταν clause: *MS* C.3.a.
καὶ .. γ᾽: "yes, and ..."
ἀφ-έστηκα: Perfect (*MS* A.3.b) of ἀφ-ίστασθαι, with genitive "stand apart, at a distance from", here of dissent: "my position is so far removed from that of ..."
οὐδὲ δοκεῖ μοι: οὐδέ, "not even", "not actually", must be linked with the infinitive σκοπεῖν: "it does not seem appropriate to me actually to be *considering* the position at the present time with regard to ..., but rather to render assistance <without discussion> ..."; then in §20 βουλεύεσθαι μέντοι (the strongly adversative μέντοι answering μέν) "while engaging in *debate* about *all* ..."

§20

δια-τηρῆσαι μή τι πάθωσι (subjunctive: *MS* C.4.b): "keep a continual watch to ensure that they do not come to any harm/ nothing untoward happens to them".
{καὶ τοῖς ... ἀποστεῖλαι: "and we must send all that they need to the soldiers who are at present there".}
ὡς with participle, "as being", "given that they are".
καθ-εστώτων: A perfect participle (*MS* A.3.b) of καθ-ίστασθαι; "have become, be" in a certain state or predicament.
ἐξ ὧν: "on what grounds".
ἵν(α) ...: Final clause, *MS* C.4.a.
πρόνοιάν ... ποιήσησθε: "exercise [literally "produce for yourselves"] some degree of forethought on your own behalf at least".
ἄρα: A somewhat wry "in the event".

ἄν (= ἐάν) clause: *MS* C.2.

τετυφῶσθαι: A perfect passive infinitive (*MS* A.4.a) of τυφοῦν, a decidedly uncomplimentary word; "be demented, non compos mentis", completely out of touch with reality. The Aristophanic term of abuse τυφο-γέρων was no doubt suggested by observation of the symptoms of senile dementia.

δοκῶ as often "be thought".

ὡς: Again with a participle, this time in the sense "as if", "as though".

προσέχητε: The element τὸν νοῦν is suppressed: "attend to, pay attention to".

§§21-25

[21-24] I leave aside the subjects of Philip's rise to power and Greece's disunity, and make this observation: when Athens, Sparta and Thebes were in positions of supremacy, their behaviour was closely watched by other states and the right of unrestricted action was denied them. Philip is allowed to treat the Greeks in a way in which the Greeks themselves were never allowed to treat one another. [25] Athens and Sparta went to war on behalf of the other states of Greece, whereas Philip has done far more wrong to the Greeks in less than thirteen years than Sparta in her thirty, or Athens in her seventy, years of supremacy.

Vocabulary
Noun
πρόγονος, ὁ   ancestor
Adjectives
ἄπιστος   mistrustful
μέτριος   moderate, reasonable, decently behaved
ταπεινός   humble
Verbs
ἐξ-αμαρτάνειν   commit an offence
παρα-λείπειν   leave on one side, pass over, omit
ἐπι-χειρεῖν   attempt (to, infin.)
συγ-χωρεῖν   concede (to, dat.)
δι-εξ-ιέναι/ -έρχομαι   enumerate, review in detail
Adverb
οὐδεπώποτε   never ever before now
Particle
ὅμως   nonetheless, nevertheless

Aids to comprehension
§21
μὲν δή (resumptive: "(well) then") is answered by ἀλλ᾽ ὁρῶ at the start of §22.

ἐκ marks the transition from a state, "from being".

τὸ κατ' ἀρχάς, "with regard to the <position> at the beginning(s)", functions as an adverbial phrase, closely with ἐκ ... ταπεινοῦ, "originally".

ηὔξηται: Perfect passive (*MS* A.4.b) of αὐξάνειν/ αὔξειν, "augment": "has grown/ risen [<so as to be> μέγας ~] to greatness".

καὶ ἀπίστως ... i.e. καὶ <ὅτι> ..., "and <the fact that> ..."

στασιαστικῶς ἔχουσι: "have factious tendencies", "are prone to divisive infighting".

πρὸς αὐτούς: "among themselves", "in their dealings with one another".

πολλῷ with a comparative, "by much" = "far".

παραδοξότερον: "more contrary to expectation" (cf. παρὰ δόξαν), "more extraordinary" that he ...

τοσοῦτον ... γενέσθαι: "grew to such stature from being [cf. ἐκ above] what he once was/ from his former <insignificant> station", ἐκεῖνος as often of what is remote in time.

ἢ ... ποιήσασθαι: "than that he should place [ποιεῖσθαι, "put" in a certain condition] under his own control all that remains into the bargain ".

ὅθ' i.e. ὅτε.

προ-είληφε: Perfect (*MS* A.3.b) of προ-λαμβάνειν, "take, acquire beforehand/ already".

ὅσα is a *quantitative* relative, here reinforced by πάντα, "all the things which", "everything that".

τοιαῦτα: "such", "in similar vein".

§22

ὁρῶ with participle, "but I do observe that ..."

συγ-κεχωρηκότας ... γεγόνασιν: Perfects, cf. *MS* A.3.a.

ὑπὲρ οὗ: No antecedent expressed: "<that> over/ in the name of which ... have taken place", "<something> which has been behind ... that have taken place".

τὸν ... χρόνον: Accusative of duration (so ... ἔτη ..., and ... χρόνους, in §23), cf. on πάντα ... χρόνον in §11: "throughout their entire history".

τὸ ποιεῖν: Articular infinitive (*MS* B), "the ability/ power to do".

καθ' ἕν' ... τῶν ῾Ελλήνων: καθ' ἕνα, "one at a time" can function as object of a verb; here (as commonly with ἕκαστος, "each and every", with which the expression is associated in §35), with dependent genitive, i.e. "the Greek peoples, one by one".

οὑτωσί (cf. on ὡδί in §3): "just like that" (spoken with a snap of the finger), without the slightest scruple.

περι-κόπτειν: "prune away all round", "pare away", hence "ravage", "lay waste".

λωποδυτεῖν: "commit λωποδυσία ["cloak-stripping", perpetrated by robbers/ muggers] (against)": "to strip/ divest them of everything they stand up in/ all they possess".

κατα-δουλοῦσθαι: Middle, "reduce them to slave-status".

ἐπ-ιόντα: "by his attacking" them, the implied accusative αὐτόν functioning as the subject of the infinitive; -ιόντα: cf. on παρ-ιόντες in §1.

§23

προστάται: "people standing in front" (~ προ-ίστασθαι with genitive "stand at the head of, be leader of"), i.e. "leading figures", "champions".

ἑβδομήκοντ᾽ ἔτη καὶ τρία (in §25, "70", cf. below "29" then "30") i.e. from 476 to 404 BC inclusive.

ἑνὸς δέοντα: Cf. on ὀλίγου δεῖν in §1; "lacking one", i.e. "thirty years save one": from 404 to 376 (battle of Naxos).

ἴσχυσαν: Aorist, "acquired power [ἰσχύς]".

τι: "to some extent/ degree".

τουτουσὶ ... χρόνους: "for these [-ί, close to us, within living memory] last periods of time", i.e. "over these last years": from 371 (battle of Leuctra) to 362 (death of Epaminondas).

ὅτι βούλοισθε: Indefinite clause in secondary sequence, *MS* D.3.

οὐδὲ πολλοῦ δεῖ: Cf. on §19. In this expression, recurrent in Demosthenes, οὐδέ does not negate what follows, but echoes the preceding concentration of negatives (οὔθ᾽ ... οὐδεπώποτ᾽): "no, far from it!".

§24

ἀλλὰ τοῦτο μέν: Cf. on §11; answered here by καὶ πάλιν, "and in their turn": "on the contrary, to take your case first, with you ..." (ὑμῖν belongs with πολεμεῖν at the end of the sentence).

μᾶλλον δέ: "but rather": we say "or rather"; again in §25.

τισιν ... προσφέρεσθαι: "their behaviour towards certain states was considered to be decidedly lacking in moderation/ wholly unreasonable" (οὐ μετρίως: stronger than "immoderately").

προσ-φέρεσθαι: "to carry oneself towards (in dealing with)", i.e. "to comport oneself" in a certain way.

οἱ μηδὲν ... αὐτοῖς (μηδέν generically): "people who had no grounds for complaint against them".

ἠδικημένων: Perfect participle passive of ἀδικεῖν, *MS* A.4.b.

ἄρξασι: Dative aorist participle, "when they had assumed the leading role".

παρ-ελθοῦσιν εἰς: "passed into", "succeeded to".

37

τὴν αὐτὴν .. ὑμῖν: The dative with ὁ αὐτός means "as"; brachylogy of a common type, "a position of supreme power the same as (exactly comparable to) you = your own".

δυναστείαν: Not a complimentary term: it suggests oligarchical rule, government under the tight control of a narrow clique.

πλεονάζειν: "exceed" a limit, "go too far" in terms of satisfying one's ambitions.

πέρα τοῦ μετρίου: "beyond what was <considered to be> moderate/ reasonable".

τὰ καθ-εστηκότ(α): Intransitive perfect participle (*MS* A.3.b) of καθ-ίστασθαι, common in the sense "established institutions", "the established order".

ἐκίνουν: Imperfect, "started to, displayed a tendency to disturb/ meddle with/ subvert".

κατέστησαν: This time (ctr. in §15) an intransitive aorist (infinitive -στῆναι), "settled, entered" into a state of war with (dative Λακεδαιμονίοις earlier).

§25

οὐδὲν ἂν ...: ἄν with participle, "although we could not from (at) the outset say".

εἰπεῖν ... ὑπ' ἀλλήλων: "say in what respect we were being wronged by one another", "point to any way in which either side was being wronged at the hands of the other".

ὧν = τούτων ἅ, the passive ἀδικεῖσθαι being this time associated with a suppressed neuter accusative (one can say ἀδικίαν or ἀδίκημα ἀδικεῖν; the corresponding passive, with "retained" accusative, is ἀδικίαν or ἀδίκημα ἀδικεῖσθαι: "because of/ to redress the wrongs which we saw the other Greek states suffering".

ἑωρῶμεν: Imperfect of ὁρᾶν: note the double augment, with retained aspiration.

ὅσ': Cf. on ὅσα in §21.

ἐξ-ημάρτηται (singular: neuter plural subject, cf. ἐστίν below): The datives following this perfect passive (*MS* A.4.b) are datives of personal agent, "by" (much more common in association with this part of the verb than ὑπό with genitive; see further on §45).

ἐλάττον(α) ... ὧν [= τούτων ἅ] ... ἠδίκηκε [perfect: *MS* A.3.b]: "less than the wrongs that ... has inflicted on".

οὐχ ὅλοις: "not whole/ entire", i.e. "in the period of less than thirteen years <during: supply ἐν> which he is (has been) on top/ has been in the ascendant".

ἐπιπολάζειν = "be on/ rise to the top/ surface". This takes us back to 353 BC, when Philip took Methone, defeated the Phocians, and threatened Thermopylae.

οὐδὲ μέρος: "not even a part", i.e. "or <I should say> rather those [the former] <do> not <constitute> so much as a fraction of these [the latter]".

38

§§26-31

[26-27] He has destroyed Olynthus, Methone, Apollonia and the thirty-two cities of Chalcidice; he has destroyed the people of Phocis; he has imposed his will on Thessaly and Euboea; he has invaded the Hellespont, having formerly marched against Ambracia; he holds Elis; lately he intrigued against Megara; his rapacity cannot be contained. [28-29] We Greeks are indifferent, and divided: entrenched in our several cities, we are incapable of standing together, or of helping one another; each is determined to make the most of his own brief respite, while his neighbour is wiped out; but nobody is so far away as to escape his onslaught. [30-31] And what kind of man is Philip? He is no true-born son of Greece, but a barbarian, and a pernicious and disreputable one at that.

Vocabulary

Nouns

κατηγορία, ἡ	accusation, denunciation
οὐσία, ἡ	substance, property
πυρετός, ὁ	fever
ἀνδράποδον, τό	slave
ἔθνος, τό	nation, people
μέμψις, ἡ	blame, censure, criticism

Adjective

γνήσιος	true-born, legitimate

Verbs

ἐπι-βουλεύειν	(with dat.) plot, intrigue against
προσ-ήκειν	belong to; be related (to, dat.), pres. partic. a person related, a relation
οἴχεσθαι	have gone, be gone, go off
περι-ορᾶν	look on, watch without concern, with indifference
σιωπᾶν	(with acc.) keep quiet about, say nothing of
ἀγνοεῖν	be ignorant, unaware of
δι-οικεῖν	manage, administer
οἰκεῖν	inhabit
τυραννεῖσθαι	be under a tyrannical mode of government
πρίασθαι	(aorist) buy, purchase
ἐν-εῖναι	be possible

Adverbs

ὠμῶς	savagely, brutally, ruthlessly

πόρρω	far off, at a distance
τήμερον	today; also ἡ τήμερον ἡμέρα
Prepositions	
ἄχρι	(with gen.) up to, until
πλησίον	(with gen.) close to, in the vicinity of

Aids to comprehension
§26

{καὶ τοῦτ᾽ ... δεῖξαι: "A few words will easily prove this".}

Ὄλυνθον... : The date of the capture of Apollonia (in Mygdonia) is not known; Olynthus: 348; Methone (west of the Thermaic Gulf): 354.

μὲν δή: Transitional, moving on to particular cases: "now then"; answered by ἀλλά (Θετταλία).

πόλεις ἐπὶ Θρᾴκης: "cities in the direction of Thrace" means "Thracian coastal cities", in this case the cities of the Chalcidic Confederation.

ἐῶ: "leave aside/ out of account"; cf. on ἐάσητε in §19.

ἀν-ῄρηκεν: Perfect of ἀν-αιρεῖν (cf. *MS* A.3.b); the perfect passive participle of this same verb presently (*MS* A.4.b).

μηδ᾽ ... εἰπεῖν: "it would not even be easy that one <supply τινα> having gone to these places should say ...", "it would not actually be an easy matter for anyone visiting these spots to say whether they had ever ..."

τοσοῦτον: "so great", "great as it was", both in general and in terms of population (22 cities).

ἀν-ῃρημένον i.e. "the extermination of ...", cf. in §§36, 56.

οὐχὶ ... παρ-ῄρηται (perfect middle-passive of παρ-αιρεῖσθαι: *MS* A.4.b): Scathingly, "has he not taken away (deprived them of) their constitutions, *and* their cities, <by robbing them of their independence through the stationing of troops there>?"

τετραρχίας: A succinct account of tetrarchies in *Oxford Classical Dictionary*, 3rd ed., p.1488.

κατ-έστησεν: Transitive (ctr. in §24) aorist of καθ-ιστάναι, "set up, establish".

ἵνα μὴ ...: Final clause, *MS* C.4.a.

κατὰ ... ἔθνη: For this use of κατά cf. the note on καθ᾽ ἕν᾽ in §22; "not .. by <whole> cities, but .. by <whole> peoples at a time", through the setting up of four distinct provincial governments.

§27

Εὐβοίᾳ: See §§57-62.

καὶ ταῦτ᾽: Cf. on §13.

Θηβῶν καὶ ᾿Αθηνῶν: They had contended for the possession of Euboea in 357 BC: both had an interest in keeping Philip out.

NOTES

διαρρήδην: "explicitly".

εἰς: "into" (cf. our "puts into his letter"), "in".

ἐμοὶ ... ἐμοῦ: Emphatic pronouns; Philip dictates to the Greeks: "and/ but [presented as an extract] as for me, *I* am at peace with people who are willing to listen to what *I* have to say!"

τοῖς ... ποιεῖ i.e. without putting what he writes into practice.

ἐφ᾿ Ἑλλήσποντον οἴχεται: One of a number of hazy references to Philip's interest in this area. He was to attack Perinthus in July 340, Byzantium in September 340.

πρότερον ...: First in a series of unconnected clauses ("asyndeton" ~ ἀ-σύν-δετον, "lacking binding links") to hammer the point home.

Ἀμβρακίαν: Mod. Arta, to the north of the Gulf of Ambracia, threatened by Philip in spring 342. The Athenians sent an expedition to Acarnania south of the Gulf in that year, to little purpose.

Ἦλιν: There was a revolution in summer 343: partisans of Philip took control.

τηλικαύτην = τοσαύτην, "such an important city"; cf. on τοσοῦτον in §26.

Μεγάροις: Cf. on §17.

ἡ βάρβαρος: Supply γῆ: "neither the Greek nor the non-Greek world".

πλεονεξίαν: πλεονεκτεῖν = "to be greedy, grasping": "his rapacious appetite" ("ambition" is too weak).

χωρεῖ: Transitively, "has room for", "is large enough to satisfy".

τἀνθρώπου = τοῦ ἀνθρώπου. ὁ ἄνθρωπος is often derogatory, "fellow, creature, character" etc.

§28
κἀγανακτοῦμεν [καὶ ἀγ-]: Here "voice our indignation", "protest angrily".

κακῶς διακείμεθα: Cf. on οὕτω διάκεισθε in §4.

δι-ορωρύγμεθα is a perfect passive of δι-ορύττειν (*MS* A.4.a), "to dig through/ across/ in between", the preverb here carrying the suggestion of separation, isolation: "we have become so entrenched/ dug in in our several cities".

συ-στῆναι: Intransitive aorist infinitive of συν-ίστασθαι: "stand/ band together, combine, unite".

κοινωνίαν ...ποιήσασθαι: "make for ourselves/ form an association of (to promote) <mutual> assistance ..."

§29
μείζω: Accusative masculine singular of the irregular comparative of μέγας, alternative form μείζονα.

τὸν χρόνον ... ἐγνωκώς (perfect participle of γιγνώσκειν: *MS* A.3.b): "because each individual has determined/ made up his mind to derive profit/ advantage

41

[κερδαίνειν ~ κέρδος, τό "gain"] from the interval during which [accusative marking duration] another <victim> is being wiped out".

ὥς γ': "as at any rate": "or so it seems to me".

οὐχ ὅπως ... πράττων: "not considering or acting how what belongs to the Greeks is going to be saved", i.e. "without considering ways or taking (practical) measures to ensure the survival of the Greek world"; cf. on πράττειν ὅπως in §1.

σωθήσεται: A future passive; singular with neuter plural subject.

ὅτι γ' ...: "of *this* fact, the fact that ..., nobody can be unaware".

περίοδος: "a going round (in a circle)" in the sense "periodic recurrence" of a condition, καταβολή a "periodic attack" (~ κατα-βάλλειν "strike down").

κακοῦ: "malady".

καὶ ... προσέρχεται: This last verb sustains the medical imagery, since it can be applied to the onset of pain: "is descending even on one who considers himself to be standing-away [perfect infinitive of ἀφ-ίστασθαι, *MS* A.3.b] now at a very great distance", i.e. "on people who think themselves at present to be situated well out of reach".

§30

καὶ μὴν κἀκεῖνό [καὶ ἐκεῖνο] γ' ἴστε: "and what is more, this is a fact that must be known to you: ..."

ἴστε: *MS* A.2.a.

ὅσα ...: On the relative cf. on ὅσα in §21; μέν is answered by ἀλλ' οὖν ... γ': "with regard to all the sufferings to which the Greeks were subjected at the hands of ..., well, they were at any rate wronged (these were at least wrongs inflicted by) people who were *genuine* <sons> of Greece".

τὸν αὐτὸν τρόπον ...: "one might have regarded this in the same light [cf. on §33] as <one> would <have> if a son ..., <considering> that he was [εἶναι] ..., but that it could not [οὐκ ἐνεῖναι be said that [ὡς] ..."

υἱὸς ... γνήσιος: "a son, born legitimate<ly>, in possession of (heir to) a considerable fortune".

γεγονώς: Perfect (active form) of γίγνεσθαι, *MS* A.3.a.

δι-ῴκει τι ...: "managed it discreditably and improperly in some way".

κατ' αὐτό .. τοῦτ' ...: On the construction see above; "he was as far as this actual thing/ aspect (i.e. the mismanagement of his affairs) was concerned ..."

κληρονόμος: "(rightful) heir".

τούτων i.e. his property.

§31

δέ γε draws a telling contrast, "but if of course".

ὑποβολιμαῖος: "a supposititious child" (~ ὑπο-βάλλεσθαι "substitute" a child).

42

ἐλυμαίνετο: A strong word, "outrage", "mutilate": "damage irreparably".

Ἡράκλεις: Vocative, a common way of saying "Good God!", "Heavens above!"

ὅσῳ: Exclamatory, "{by} how much ..."

ἔφησαν: Cf. on φησάντων in §1.

ὧν i.e. τούτων ἅ.

οὐχ οὕτως ἔχουσιν: "they do not have such an attitude": the negative οὐχ is repeated for emphasis: "no they do not!".

οὐ μόνον ...: Translate the participles by means of a concessive clause: "though ..."

ἐντεῦθεν ὅθεν ...: "from a place whence <it is> honourable/ creditable to say <one comes>", i.e. "from a country which one may decently/ without a blush claim as one's own".

ὀλέθρου Μακεδόνος: ὄλεθρος, "(act of) destruction", here as commonly of a person, "agent of destruction": "a pernicious Macedonian".

ὅθεν: "from where" = "from which country", to be extracted from the preceding Μακεδόνος.

σπουδαῖον: "of good/ decent quality", "respectable".

ἦν for ἐξῆν, πρότερον i.e. "it used not to be possible ..."

§§32-35

[32] His insolence knows no bounds: the destroyer of Greek cities presides over the Pythian Games. [33-35] He is arbiter of Thessaly and Euboea. Yet the Greeks look on as they would watch a hailstorm! He also gets away with wronging the various peoples of Greece, the Corinthians, the Achaeans, the Thebans; he is threatening Byzantium; he is occupying Cardia. And what do we do?

Vocabulary

Noun

ἀγών -ῶνος, ὁ	(national) meeting-ground (for viewing the great games), national venue

Verbs

ἐκ-βάλλειν	expel
μέλλειν	delay, be dilatory
ἀν-έχεσθαι	hold up, endure
εὔχεσθαι	pray
πολιτεύεσθαι	be governed
ἀπιστεῖν	(with dat.) distrust
θεωρεῖν	gaze at, view (like a spectator at the games)
παρα-διδόναι	hand over

Adverb
ἀσελγῶς   with the violence/ brutality of a bully
Preposition
πρός   (with dat.) in addition to

Aids to comprehension
§32
τί ... ἀπολείπει; The verb is used intransitively, with genitive: "in what respect
  does he fall short of extreme hybris?", i.e. "does his outrageous behaviour know
  any bounds?"
πρός ... ἀν-ῃρηκέναι: Articular infinitive (*MS* B), perfect form (*MS* A.3.b): "on
  top of his having wiped out cities".
τίθησι: "sets up" = "assumes the role of director/ president of". Philip presided at
  the Pythian Games in person in 346 and through a deputy in 342.
τῶν ' Ελλήνων: Philip is *not* a Greek.
κἄν for καὶ ἐάν, *MS* C.2.
δούλους: Cuttingly: Philip is a king, his subjects (however highly placed) are his
  slaves.
ἀγωνοθετήσοντας: Future participle expressing purpose (so also in §33
  ἐκβαλοῦντας, καταστήσοντας), "to preside at the event".
{κύριος ... μέτεστι; "Is he not master of Thermopylae, and of the passes which
  lead into Hellenic territory? Does he not hold that district with garrisons and
  mercenaries? Has he not taken the precedence in consulting the oracle, and
  thrust aside ourselves and the Thessalians and Dorians and the rest of the
  Amphictyons, though the right is not one which is given even to all of the
  Hellenes?"}

§33
γράφει (supply a prefatory negative from §32 init.: likewise for the succeeding
  questions): "issues written instructions as to".
ὃν .. τρόπον: "in what way", "how"; cf. τὸν αὐτὸν τρόπον shortly.
ξένους (cf. on §58): Again in the sense "mercenaries".
Πορθμόν: The port of Eretria.
δῆμον: "popular/ democratic party".
Φιλιστίδην: See on §59.
καταστήσοντας: Cf. on κατέστησεν in §26.
τὴν χάλαζαν: (just as they <can only> gaze at) "the hail" (falling before their very
  eyes).
θεωρεῖν: Supply "these events".

καθ' ἑαυτοὺς .. γενέσθαι: "occur in relation to themselves", i.e. "fall where they are".

ἕκαστοι: The several peoples of Greece.

§34

δ': Cf. on μὴ παθεῖν δ' in §13.

ἐφ' οἷς ...: "<in cases> in which Greece suffers outrages at his hands".

ὧν = τούτων ἅ, "fights back over/ in retaliation for the wrongs to which each is personally (αὐτός) subjected"; cf. on ἀδικεῖσθαι in §25.

τοῦτο ... ἐστιν: "it is this now that is the most extreme [~ τὸ ἔσχατον] thing", i.e. "with this [the multiplicity of wrongs committed against individuals] we come to the most extreme aspect <of his outrageous behaviour>" (cf. τῆς ἐσχάτης ὕβρεως applied to Philip in §32): an account of his treatment of individual states follows.

Κορινθίων: Thrown forward for emphasis, as are the other possessive genitives Ἀχαιῶν, Θηβαίων, ἡμῶν: "Ambracia and Leucas belong to Corinth: has he not ...?" and so on. Leucas: an island off the coast of Acarnania. Both it and Ambracia were Corinthian colonies.

ἐλήλυθε: Perfect of ἰέναι/ ἔρχομαι (MS A.3.a); ὀμώμοκεν, of ὀμνύναι (ibid.) [with future infinitive]; ἀφ-ῄρηται, of ἀφ-αιρεῖσθαι (MS A.4.b).

Ναύπακτον: On the north side of the Gulf of Corinth, colonised by Achaea in 367 and given to Aetolia in 338.

Ἐχῖνον: A Theban colony in Thessaly, on the north coast of the Malian Gulf.

συμμάχους ὄντας: "who are his allies" (and had been since the year 351).

§35

ἐῶ τἆλλα [τὰ ἄλλα], ἀλλὰ ...: "I leave aside [cf. on ἐῶ in §26] the others, but ...", i.e. "— not to mention all the others —".

Καρδίαν: Cf. on §16.

μαλκίομεν: "suffer from μάλκη, numbness brought on by extreme cold": "act as if thoroughly benumbed, be in a state of torpor". μαλκίομεν is recorded as a variant reading by the lexicographer Harpocration: μαλακιζόμεθα, a bland "we act soft [~ adj. μαλακός], like cowards", is preferred by many.

πρὸς ... βλέπομεν: "we look <suspiciously> in the direction of/ eye our neighbours" (instead of keeping an eye on Philip).

χρώμενον: χρῆσθαι with dative, "use", often "treat" a person in a certain way.

ἐπειδάν with aorist subjunctive: MS C.3.a.

καθ' ἕν': Cf. on §22.

τί ποιήσειν: This second τί harks back to the irate τί οἴεσθε after the train of thought has been interrupted by the indefinite clause: we might translate "what, once he has ..., what do you think ...?"

45

§§36-40

[36-39] The desire for freedom, and the spirit that defeated the Persians, are with us no more. Outlooks have changed: it used to be the case that those in the pay of our national enemies were detested and severely punished. Whereas nothing affecting our vital interests could be bought, nowadays everything is sold on the open market; corruption is rife. [40] Our material resources have greatly increased — but that advantage is negated by these traffickers.

Vocabulary
Nouns

αἰτία, ἡ	cause, reason
ἀφθονία, ἡ	abundance, plenty
διάνοια, ἡ	mind, thought (-processes), mental make-up; [§43] intention
ναυμαχία, ἡ	sea-battle, naval engagement
ὁμόνοια, ἡ	unanimity, concord
τιμωρία, ἡ	vengeance, punishment, penalty
ζῆλος, ὁ	envy
μῖσος, τό	hatred, odium
πλῆθος, τό	great number, quantity, amount
τριήρης, ἡ	trireme, warship
γέλως -ωτος, ὁ	laughter, derision

Adjective

πεζός	on land, land-

Verbs

ἐλέγχειν	in passive, be convicted
κολάζειν	chastise
ἐπι-τιμᾶν	(with dat.) censure, criticise
ἡττᾶσθαι	(with gen.) be less/ weaker than, no match for; be worsted, defeated in
ἀμελεῖν	be careless, negligent
δωροδοκεῖν	take bribes
μισεῖν	hate, detest
πωλεῖν	sell, put up for sale

Adverb

ὅλως	altogether; οὐχ ὅλως not at all

Preposition

ἄνευ
(with gen.) without; ἄνευ λόγου without (the exercise of) reason, irrationally

Aids to comprehension
§36

τουτων-ί: "these present ills".

οὔτε τόθ' ... οὔτε νῦν: That is to say, just as it was not without ... that the Greeks in days gone by were so eager for freedom, so it cannot be without ... that the present-day Greeks are so eager for slave-status.

εἶχον: Note the irregular augment.

τὸ δουλεύειν: Articular infinitive, *MS* B.

ἦν ...: Asyndeton as the speaker offers weighty reflections on the good old days; animated repetition (ἦν, "there was some thing/ some principle ..., there really was").

τῶν πολλῶν: "the peoples" of Greece.

ἐλευθέραν ἦγε τὴν Ἑλλάδα: "was successful in maintaining [ἄγειν, "keep", like δι-άγειν] Greece's freedom", or "in leading Greece along freedom's path".

ἀπολωλός: "but now it having been lost has ...", i.e. "the loss/ obliteration of which today has ..."; perfect participle: *MS* A.3.a.

λελύμανται: Perfect middle-passive of λυμαίνεσθαι (*MS* A.4.a), cf. on ἐλυμαίνετο in §31: "has completely ruined".

ἄνω καὶ κάτω πεποίηκε (perfect: *MS* A.3.a): "has rendered/ put up and down" = "has turned the affairs of Greece/ the Greek world upside-down".

§37

{οὐδὲν ... ὅτι: "It was nothing subtle or clever, but simply that"}

χαλεπώτατον: "very difficult to confront", i.e. "having the most serious consequences" for the culprit.

τὸ δωροδοκοῦντ(α) ἐλεγχθῆναι: Articular infinitive with accusative serving as subject (*MS* B), "the - one receiving a bribe - to be convicted", "a conviction for taking a bribe" (... τοῦτον, "the guilty party").

{καὶ παραίτησις ... συγγνώμη: "there could be no plea for mercy, nor hope of pardon".}

§38

τὸν οὖν καιρὸν ...: "the critical moment for action in any given case, the moment which fortune often contrives to put men's way — even men who are negligent, to the detriment of those who are vigilant — it was not possible to purchase

from (public) speakers ~ politicians ...": προσεχόντων: cf. on προσέχητε in
§20; ἦν = ἐξῆν.

τὴν ... ὁμόνοιαν: "our [Greek] mutual concord".

§39

ἅπανθ᾽ ... ταῦτα: "all these <high principles>" underlying the refusal to "sell" just
outlined.

ἐκ-πέπραται/ ἀντ-εισ-ῆκται (singulars, neuter plural subjects: cf. below ἐστί,
ἤρτηται; §40 ἐστί, γίγνεται): Perfect passives (*MS* A.4.a/b). The former: "have
been sold and (ἐκ-) exported like <goods> from (on) the open market"; the
latter: "have been imported in their stead", suppressed subject ταῦτα (ὑφ᾽ ὧν ...).

ἀπόλωλε/ νενόσηκεν: Perfects: *MS* A.3.a; for the νόσος image (here more radical)
cf. νοσοῦσι in §12: "is ruined and diseased", i.e. "has been/ is stricken with a
terminal disease".

εἴληφε: Perfect of λαμβάνειν (*MS* A.3.b), "has taken something" (ref. to
δωροδοκία shortly).

ἄν (= ἐάν) with subjunctive: *MS* C.2; "if he confesses".

{συγγνώμη τοῖς ἐλεγχομένοις: "pardon granted to those whose guilt is proved".}

τούτοις: Neuter, this behaviour.

τἄλλα: τὰ ἄλλα.

ὅσ(α): Cf. on §21.

ἐκ ... ἤρτηται: Perfect passive (*MS* A.4.b) of ἀρτᾶν, "hang", "suspend", hence in
passive with ἐκ "depend on": "all the other <malpractices/ vices> that are
attendant upon bribe-taking".

τοῦ δωροδοκεῖν: Articular infinitive, *MS* B.

§40

ἐπεὶ .. γε: "<this is where the shortfall is to be found,> because as far as warships
go at any rate, and ...; *but* ..."

σωμάτων πλῆθος ...: "large quantity of bodies ...", i.e. "ample supply of able-
bodied men and money".

τῆς ἄλλης κατασκευῆς: "the rest of the materials", that is "material resources/
assets in general".

τἄλλ᾽ οἷς ἄν ... κρίνοι: "all the other things by which one might judge the cities to
be strong", i.e. "all the other indicators of the power wielded by the cities of
Greece".

ἅπασι: "every one of us".

πλείω/ μείζω: Comparatives of πολύς and μέγας respectively, alternative
termination -ονα.

τῶν τότε: Compendiously for "than was available to our counterparts in former
times".

πολλῷ with comparative, "by far" (cf. in §21); put last for emphasis.

ταῦτ᾽ ... γίγνεται: A final flourish, with three negative adjectives in asyndeton, no
doubt intoned with a Churchillian solemnity and sense of occasion: "these
<resources> are rendered *un*serviceable, *un*availing, *un*profitable through the
operations of those who traffic in them!"

§§41-46

*[41-44] Things were different in the days of our forefathers: on one occasion, an
individual who brought the gold of Persia into the Peloponnese was declared an
outlaw by Athens. [45] The result of such punishment was that Greece was
formidable to the barbarian, not the barbarian to Greece. [46] What are your
sentiments about corruption and related offences* now? *Shall I tell you and will
you not be angry?*

Vocabulary
Nouns

σωτηρία, ἡ	safety, preservation, security
στήλη, ἡ	slab, tablet (inscribed, for public display)
μάρτυς -υρος, ὁ	witness

Adjectives

ἐναντίος	opposite
καθαρός	pure, free from (the) pollution (of homicide)
χαλκοῦς -ῆ -οῦν	[contracted: χάλκεος etc.] (made of) bronze

Verbs

δια-φθείρειν	destroy; spoil, corrupt, suborn
δικάζεσθαι	go to law
ὀργίζεσθαι	be, get angry
διακονεῖν	(with dat.) serve (a master)
προσ-δεῖσθαι	(with gen.) need in addition, require further
ὠνεῖσθαι	buy (a thing, or a person)
κατα-τίθεσθαι	deposit

Adverb

εἰκότως	reasonably, naturally enough

Particle

οὐκοῦν	so, accordingly

Aids to comprehension

§41

ἔχει: Singular with neuter plural subject: cf. ἐγένετο and ἐστί in §42.

τὰ μὲν νῦν ... τὰ δ' ἐν ...: "with regard to the present state of affairs ... but with regard to the position/ attitudes in earlier times [ἄνωθεν like ἄνω simply "formerly", "of old"] ..."

τἀναντί᾽ [τὰ ἐναντία, here adverbial] εἶχεν: "the opposite was the case".

γράμματα: "letters" = "inscribed/ written record".

ἀκεῖνοι: ἃ ἐκεῖνοι.

εἰς ["on"] στήλην .. γράψαντες: Cf. on §27.

ἀκρόπολιν: Without article; so commonly πόλις, ἄστυ, ἀγορά.

{οὐχ ... γράμματα: "not to be a lesson to themselves — they needed no such record to put them in a right mind — but to be a reminder and an example to you of the zeal that you ought to display in such a cause. What then is the record?"}

§42

On the various accounts of Arthmius see R. Meiggs, *The Athenian Empire* (Oxford, 1972), 508-12.

Πυθώνακτος: "<son> of Pythonax", an element very commonly omitted in the stereotyped Athenian method of *citizen*-identification: name, father's name, demotic.

ἄτιμος: "dishonoured", here in the technical sense "divested of one's rights", by which is generally meant deprivation of one's civil rights, disfranchisement: the exact complexion of the ἀτιμία imposed in this particular case is going to be elucidated in §44.

εἶθ᾽: εἶτα, "then".

γέγραπται (again in §44): Perfect passive, *MS* A.4.a.

ἤγαγεν: Imperfective (strong) aorist of ἄγειν.

§43

δή with imperative, here an urgent "please", "I must ask you to".

ποθ᾽: ποτε with (here indirect) interrogative means "ever", "on earth", sim.: "just what their intention was".

ἀξίωμα: Various renderings are on offer: probably "their conception of their duty", the course they thought worthy (~ ἀξιοῦν) of themselves as citizens of Athens.

δοῦλον: Cf. on §32; note δεσπότη presently.

βασιλέως: Cf. on §16.

Ζέλεια: A town in the Troad.

τῆς Ἀσίας: "belonging to/ in Asia".

χρυσίον: Previously χρυσόν, "gold"; now χρυσίον, "gold coin".

ἐχθρόν: "personal enemy", an even more invidious term than the previous πολέμιος, "public enemy".

ἀν-έγραψαν: "recorded him as being ... by means of a public inscription".

ἀτίμους: Supply ἀνέγραψαν; plural = himself + family-members (γένος).

§44

οὐχ ἦν ...: "not which deprivation of rights one would speak of in the particular way that one does [cf. on ὡδί in §3]", i.e. "not deprivation of rights in the sense that we would normally assign to that procedure".

φήσειεν: Cf. on φησάντων in §1.

τί .. τῷ ...; "what <was> it to ...?", "how could it matter to ...?"

τῶν Ἀθηναίων κοινῶν [thrown forward, juxtaposed to τῷ Ζελείτῃ] ... ἔμελλεν; "if it was from a share in the common rights of *Athenians* that he was to be excluded?"

ἐν τοῖς ... νόμοις: "in the laws relating to homicide".

ὑπὲρ ὧν [i.e. ὑπὲρ τούτων ὑπὲρ ὧν] ... δικάσασθαι: "with reference to those [whoever they might be: indefinite clause with subjunctive: *MS* C.3.a] in whose case he does not grant the right to go to law with/ bring cases involving homicide (to prosecute for homicide)". "He" is the framer of the laws/ legislator, the subject of φησί below; for διδόναι with infinitive cf. in §55; genitive φόνου = "for/ over homicide".

{ἀλλ' ... ἀποκτεῖναι "but <where> the slaying of them is to be a holy act".}

φησί takes over from γέγραπται.

τεθνάτω: A perfect third person singular imperative (*MS* A.3.a) imparting a suggestion of finality, irrevocability: "let him die", "he must die" — such an offender can be slain with impunity: that is what ἀτιμία means in the case of Arthmius and his like.

τοῦτο .. λέγει: "this is what <the legislator> means, that ...".

δή: "then", or "of course".

τούτων τιν': "any of these people", the plural recalling (ὑπὲρ) ὧν earlier.

§45

ἐπιμελητέον εἶναι: A verbal adjective (~ ἐπι-μελεῖσθαι, with genitive, "take care of"), "that it was necessary for themselves to devote attention to ..." (the dative is normal with this part of speech to express personal agency, cf. in §§70, 74), i.e. "that the safety of *all* Greeks was their personal concern/ responsibility".

οὐ .. ἂν αὐτοῖς ἔμελ': For μέλειν cf. on §16; "it would not concern them if/ they would not care whether ..."

μὴ τοῦτο ὑπολαμβάνουσιν: Dative plural participle, in agreement with αὐτοῖς, with conditional force (note μή): "if not supposing this thing", i.e. "unless they assumed this to be the case".

ἐκόλαζον ...: That is to say, they carried the processes of corrective [κόλασις] and retributive [τιμωρία] punishment so far as actually to make the offenders στηλῖται, "having their names inscribed/ advertised on a stele", with all the ignominy that that entailed, both immediately and in the longer term.

οὓς αἴσθοιντο: Indefinite clause in secondary sequence: *MS* D.3.

ἐκ: "as a result of".

τὰ τῶν Ἑλλήνων: "the Greek world", "the Greeks and all they stood for".

§46

ὑμεῖς: Emphatic: present-day Athenians simply did not reflect the attitudes and concerns of their great predecessors.

τἄλλα: τὰ ἄλλα.

{ἴστ' ... τίνος; "You know it yourselves; for why should I accuse you explicitly on every point? And that [i.e. the attitude] of the rest of the Hellenes is like your own, and no better; and so I say that the present situation demands our utmost earnestness and good counsel. What counsel?"}

εἴπω κελεύετε; Deliberative subjunctive (*MS* C.5(i)), "am I to tell you, do you <so> instruct?": "if you have no objections, I shall tell you".

[ΕΚ ΤΟΥ ΓΡΑΜΜΑΤΕΙΟΥ ΑΝΑΓΙΓΝΩΣΚΕΙ]: If a "document" was read out what could its purport have been? This heading, present in a number of important MSS, is generally excised by modern editors. It does look however as if *something* has dropped out of the text here, since the close of §46 leads one to expect some forthright pronouncements on the subject of Athenian slackness. It may be that perusal of the "other version", ἴστε κτλ. (see above), which excludes a long tirade, has led someone to trim the text at his point.

§§47-52

[47-50] We are assured by some that we are exaggerating Philip's power: it is less than that of Sparta which we succeeded in resisting. But consider recent developments in the techniques of waging war. Before there were just summer campaigns, heavy-armed citizen troops, and no bribery: the waging of war was an open business. Now treachery is rampant; pitched battles are a thing of the past; Philip's successes are due to his deployment of mobile light troops, and to the use of siege-engines; and he fights all the year round. [51-52] We must keep Philip at a distance, and avoid a pitched battle, for which we are much less well prepared than for plundering his territory in war.

NOTES

Vocabulary
Nouns

ψιλοί, οἱ	light-armed troops
τοξόται, οἱ	archers
ἱππεῖς, οἱ	cavalry(men)
χώρα, ἡ	land, territory
ὥρα, ἡ	season
προδότης, ὁ	traitor
φύσις, ἡ	nature
θέρος, τό	summer
χειμών -ῶνος, ὁ	winter
μήν μηνός, ὁ	month
Adjectives	
ἀρχαῖος	old-fashioned, antiquated
μυρίος	countless, innumerable
Verbs	
ἐμ-βάλλειν	intransitive, mount an invasion, invade
προσ-πίπτειν	(πρός, with acc.) fall upon, launch an attack on
δι-αγωνίζεσθαι	engage in a decisive struggle
ἀνα-χωρεῖν	withdraw, retire
πολιορκεῖν	lay siege to, besiege
παρα-μυθεῖσθαι	comfort, reassure
κακοῦν	maltreat, injure, ravage
ὑφ-ίστασθαι	withstand, be capable of resistance to

Aids to comprehension
§47

ὡς ἄρ' ...: (there is an argument) "to the effect that Philip, after all/ when all is said and done ..."

οἷοι: οἷος is a *qualitative* relative, "the kind of person (etc.) who ...", often (though not here) prefaced with a τοιοῦτος: "Philip's position is not yet comparable to that once enjoyed by ..."

βασιλέα: Cf. on §16; emphatically placed ("..., no less"), as is θαλάττης: effectively "the sea in addition to the entire land area", the latter being their traditional power-base, the former that of her arch-rivals.

ἠμύνατο: Here with accusative, "defend oneself against".

κἀκείνους: καὶ ἐκείνους.

ἀν-ηρπάσθη: ἀν-αρπάζειν, "snatch up <and carry away>", hence figuratively in the passive "be swept away", "engulfed".

53

ἁπάντων ὡς ἔπος εἰπεῖν: As usual this infinitival expression (cf. in §1) softens the force of a quantitative term, "so to speak" ~ "virtually/just about" every.

πολλὴν εἰληφότων ἐπίδοσιν: εἰληφότων is perfect participle of λαμβάνειν (*MS* A.3.b), "assume", ἐπίδοσις means "advance, improvement, progress" (~ ἐπιδιδόναι, intransitively, "increase, advance, develop", cf. below): "whereas/ although there have been [first of two genitives absolute] considerable advances in practically every sphere".

οὐδὲν ... τοῖς πρότερον: "whereas/ although the things now in no way resemble the things before", i.e. "... <in consequence> the world of today is radically different from that of yesterday".

τὰ τοῦ πολέμου: "the science of war", "techniques of warfare".

κεκινῆσθαι/ ἐπι-δεδωκέναι: On the perfects see *MS* A.4.a/3.a; κινεῖσθαι here bears the sense "be altered radically/ revolutionised".

§48

ἀκούω: "I know from what I have been told", "am informed that".

... μῆνας ...: Accusative marking duration.

τὴν ὡραίαν αὐτήν: "<that is,> just for the actual summer- (~ campaigning-) season" (cf. ὥρα in §50).

ἂν ... ἀναχωρεῖν: "would [cf. on ἄν in §1] ... return": this is an instance of the indirect version of ἄν with imperfect to express repeated action ("iterative" imperfect).

ὁπλίταις ...: Datives: "by means of" = "with".

πολιτικοῖς στρατεύμασιν: "citizen-armies/ troops" (rather than mercenaries).

ἐπ᾽ with genitive, "in the direction of".

μᾶλλον δέ: Cf. on §24.

πολιτικῶς (οὕτως εἶχον): "they behaved so much like polis-members", "they were so true to the ideals of the Greek state".

οὐδὲ ... οὐδενὸς οὐδέν: Not the oblique μηδέ etc., despite the infinitival construction; there is stress on the *fact* that such shady practices were unknown.

χρημάτων: For the genitive cf. on §9.

εἶναι νόμιμόν ...: "was of a legitimate [fairly and properly regulated according to the accepted "rules of the game"] and wholly open kind" (τις with adjective: ἄδικός τις εἶ, "you're a dishonest sort of chap/ type").

§49

τὰ πλεῖστα ... ἀπολωλεκότας (perfect participle: *MS* A.3.a): "the most things the traitors (as) having ruined", i.e. "that most of our past losses/ disasters have been due to acts of treachery".

ἐκ ... μάχης: "as a result of marshalling of troops or battle", that is, "as a result of fighting regular pitched/ set battles".

54

ἀκούετε with participle as ἀκούω in §48, "that ..."

οὐχὶ τῷ ... ἄγειν: Articular infinitive (*MS* B), "not <just> by virtue of the fact that he leads heavy infantry in phalanx-formation", followed up with a second, τῷ ... ἐξ-ηρτῆσθαι (perfect: *MS* A.4.b; cf. on §39: here scornfully "have hung upon/ attached to oneself"): "by having equipped himself with ..."

τοιοῦτον .. στρατόπεδον: "<and> similar fighting men/ troops".

§50

ἐπειδάν with subjunctive: *MS* C.3.a.

ἐπὶ τούτοις: "in command of/ at the head of" these fighting men.

νοσοῦντας ἐν αὐτοῖς: Cf. on §12; "people suffering from/ in the throes of internal disorder/ faction".

ἀπιστίαν i.e. of one another.

ἐξ-ίῃ: Cf. on παριόντες in §1; "goes out" = "is prepared to take the field".

ὡς οὐδὲν διαφέρει: "that they do not differ at all", i.e. I pass over the fact that he draws no distinction between summer and winter.

ἐξαίρετος: "taken/ picked out", hence "excepted, set apart".

δια-λείπει: Subject Philip: "during which he leaves an interval", "suspends operations".

§51

εἰδότας: *MS* A.2.a.

προσ-έσθαι: This is aorist middle infinitive of προσ-ιέναι/ -ίημι, "admit", "let ... penetrate into the (our) territory (our homeland, Attica)".

εὐήθειαν: "simplicity", "uncomplicated (and guileless) tactics" adopted in that conflict.

ἐκ-τραχηλισθῆναι: Uncompromising language: "to have one's neck [τράχηλος] <bent back and> snapped" (as might happen in a no-holds-barred wrestling-match, cf. the image below).

ὡς ἐκ πλείστου: ὡς goes with πλείστου, "as ... as possible", i.e. "(be on your guard against him/ take precautions to deal with him) from/ at the greatest possible distance".

τοῖς ... παρασκευαῖς: "with your <political> measures and with your preparations <to meet the military crisis>".

ὅπως .. μὴ .. σκοποῦντας with future: cf. on §1.

κινήσεται: "will stir (himself)" from his home-base.

συμ-πλακέντας: συμ-πλέκεσθαι, "be twined together", hence "be locked together" (like wrestlers).

§52

φύσει closely with πλεονεκτήμαθ' (-ατα), "natural advantages" (~ πλεονεκτεῖν "gain an advantage", "have the edge").

ὑπ-άρχει: "are at our disposal"; singular with neuter plural subject.

ἄν περ i.e. ἐάν περ (cf. *MS* C.2) "if really/ only".

ἄγειν καὶ φέρειν (drive off, round up cattle, slaves etc. and carry off anything not nailed down): A set phrase for "harry", "ravage".

ἔστι for ἔξεστι.

κακῶς ποιεῖν: Cf. κακοῦν in §48.

ἄλλα μυρία: "<and> ..."

ἀγῶν(α): "bout, match, set-to", often in the military sphere: "a <single> pitched battle", on the outcome of which the whole issue would be decided.

ἤσκηται: Perfect passive of ἀσκεῖν (*MS* A.4.b), an agonistic term in the sense "exercise, train": "he is better trained ..."

§§53-55

But before you can conquer your enemy abroad, you must punish his supporters at home. And yet, though some of them could not deny that they are in his pay, you listen to them and derive amusement from what they say, and afford them greater immunity than those who speak in your own interests.

Vocabulary
Nouns

ἀσφάλεια, ἡ	safety, security
λοιδορία, ἡ	(verbal) abuse, invective ~ λοιδορεῖσθαι (aorist λοιδορηθῆναι; with dat.) abuse, inveigh against
μωρία, ἡ	(criminal) folly, stupidity, obtuseness
παράνοια, ἡ	derangement, insanity
σκῶμμα σκώμματος, τό	(vulgar) jest(ing), ribaldry
Verbs	
πολιτεύεσθαι	engage in political activities
ἀκροᾶσθαι	(with gen.) lend an ear to, listen to
θεᾶσθαι	behold, observe
ὑπηρετεῖν	(with dat.) serve, be an underling of
ἀρνεῖσθαι	(aorist ἀρνηθῆναι) deny
ἐν-θυμεῖσθαι	reflect (on), consider
Asseverative particle	
μά	(with accus.) used in swearing "by" a deity

Aids to comprehension

§53

δέ: Cf. on μὴ παθεῖν δ᾽ in §13.

ταῦτα γιγνώσκειν: "to decide on these steps" (specified in §51-52).

οὐδέ: "nor even"; supply μόνον δεῖ.

τοῖς ἔργοις ... τοῖς τοῦ πολέμου: "by <actually> putting into effect measures to prosecute the war" (according to the tactics just advocated).

ἐκεῖνον ἀμύνεσθαι: Cf. on §47.

καὶ τῷ λογισμῷ καὶ τῇ διανοίᾳ: "in line with both reasoning and feelings", that is, "on both rational and moral grounds".

παρ᾽ ὑμῖν: Here, in the ecclesia.

μισῆσαι: Aorist infinitive, "to come out with/ show your detestation of".

πρὶν ἄν with aorist subjunctive, "until one has ...": *MS* C.3.b.

§54

ὑμεῖς with telling emphasis: "*you* <being the kind you are>".

εἰς τοῦτ᾽: Cf. in §1; "you have reached this point = such a pitch of ..."; picked up by ὥστε ...

ἀφ-ῖχθε: Perfect: *MS* A.4.b.

οὐκ ἔχω τί λέγω: He breaks off with an exasperated "I do not know what to call it!"; λέγω "deliberative" subjunctive: *MS* C.5(i). Here, as so often elsewhere, Demosthenes deplores the fact that those who attend deliberative meetings of the Assembly, like jurors in the law-courts, find abusive oratory good entertainment.

ἐπ-ελήλυθε (perfect of ἐπ-ιέναι/ -έρχομαι: *MS* A.3.a): Impersonally, "it has entered my head, occurred" to me.

καί: "actually" to entertain the fear that what is happening may not be explicable in normal terms.

μή ... ἐλαύνῃ: On the use of the subjunctive see *MS* C.4.b.

τι δαιμόνιον: "some <malign> supernatural power may be driving (~ controlling, or better plaguing, of deliberate persecution) our affairs/ fortunes".

λοιδορίας ... αἰτίας: The governing preposition is expressed only with the last item in this string of genitives; in the case of the first three "for the sake of/ because of" means "in order to satisfy your desire for/ be diverted by".

φθόνου: "(displays of) malice/ spite".

ἧστινος ... αἰτίας: Indefinite clause (*MS* C.3.a), "from whatever motive you happen <to be acting thus>" i.e. "— or whatever your motive may be —".

ἀνθρώπους μισθωτούς: "hired men/ people (ἄνθρωπος contemptuously) who are in his pay" (cf. on §14).

ὡς οὐκ εἰσί: Cf. the redundant use of the negative in the common ἀρνεῖσθαι μή + infinitive.

ἄν i.e. ἐάν (cf. *MS* C.2), "if ... some people" = "whenever ... people".

§55

καὶ ... ὂν δεινόν: "and this is not as yet [in comparison with what is to follow] serious, though it *is* [participle in emphatic position] serious" is a way of saying "serious as this is, and it *is* serious, there is worse to come: why, you have actually ...!"

δεδώκατε: Perfect (*MS* A.3.a), διδόναι with infinitive (cf. in §44) = "you have granted them the power to ..."

ὅσας: "how many", "the multitude of ... which ..."; cf. on §21.

παρα-σκευάζει: "provides", "creates".

τὸ ... ἐθέλειν: Articular infinitive: *MS* B.

λέξω .. ἔργα: "I will state actual facts".

εἴσεσθε: Future of εἰδέναι.

§§56-58

Consider the cases of Olynthus and Eretria.

Vocabulary
Noun
ἔθος, τό	habit, practice
Adjectives	
ταλαίπωρος	sorely tried, thoroughly wretched
δυστυχής	luckless, unfortunate
Verbs	
ἀπ-αλλάττεσθαι	(aor. ἀπ-αλλαγῆναι) be got rid of
ἐργάζεσθαι	(aor. ἐργάσασθαι, tense εἰργ-) effect, carry out, cause
ἐξ-ολλύναι	destroy, ruin (completely)
προ-διδόναι	betray
Adverbs	
ἄλλοθι	elsewhere
οὐδαμοῦ	nowhere

Aids to comprehension
§56
τῶν ἐν τοῖς πράγμασι (cf. in §2): "of those <active> in politics/ those in government".

Φιλίππου: "of Ph." = "on Ph.'s side", his supporters/ partisans.

πάνθ': "in all respects, in everything".

τοῦ βελτίστου: "of the best" (cf. on τοῦ Φιλίππου above) ~ "who had their city's best interests at heart", true patriots, cf. τοὺς τὰ βέλτιστα λέγοντας below.

ὅπως μὴ ... πράττοντες: Cf. on §1.

πότεροι = "which of two parties?"

δή: Insistently, "tell me now".

ἱππέας: A body of 500 men, betrayed into Philip's hands by their own officers.

προὕδοσαν: Internal contraction, for προ-έδοσαν.

ὧν προδοθέντων: Genitive absolute, "who having been betrayed", i.e. "the betrayal of whom spelled ruin for ..."

οἱ τὰ Φιλίππου φρονοῦντες: Cf. on §18.

ἦν: "<still> existed".

συκοφαντοῦντες καὶ διαβάλλοντες: "maliciously prosecuting and misrepresenting": a συκοφάντης is a professional informer/ prosecutor who sets out to "get" people by bringing (in the perception of the victim and/ or of others not directly involved) baseless charges out of malevolent and self-seeking motives.

οὕτως, ὥστε: "so effectively that".

τόν γ' Ἀπολλωνίδην: The particle is there to arrest the attention: "Apollonides, yes Ap."; leader of the democratic party, see in §66.

καί: "actually".

§57

τοίνυν: Here continuative, "now".

πάντα κάκ': "nothing but/ utter ruin".

ἀλλ' ...: Events of 342/1.

τῶν ξένων: An appendage to the single subject of the participle (genitive absolute), "Pl. ... together with his mercenaries".

Πορθμόν: Cf. on §33.

ἐφ' ὑμᾶς ... πράγματα: "wanted to put [imperfect] the government into your hands/ under your control".

τούτων: "the latter".

τὰ πολλά: A set phrase, "for the most part", "in the main", followed up with τὰ πάνθ', "on all counts", "exclusively".

μᾶλλον δέ: Cf. on §24.

τελευτῶντες: "ending up", where we would say "in the end", "ultimately".

§58

καὶ γάρ τοι: This run of particles can express a result, "and in consequence", but here rather there is a causal connection (the reason why the Eretrians merited the labels ταλαίπωροι and δυστυχεῖς): "because the fact is, don't forget, that ..."

59

πέμψας ... ξένους: We have only Demosthenes' word for it that Philip supplied these mercenaries. But it is hard to believe that he was just an idle observer.

ὁ σύμμαχος αὐτοῖς: Sarcastic; dative after συμ-.

περι-εῖλε: "took (away) all round" = "pulled down the surrounding ..."

κατέστησε: Cf. on §26.

Κλείταρχον: The foremost pro-Macedonian of Eretria, expelled by a force under the Athenian general Phocion in the autumn of 341.

ἐξ-ελήλακεν: Perfect, *MS* A.3.a; object the Eretrian democrats.

δὶς ἤδη: With ἐξελήλακεν, "and subsequent to this he has ... on two occasions already".

σῴζεσθαι: That is, from the clutches of Philip's partisans.

{τότε ... Παρμενίωνος: "sending on the first occasion the mercenaries commanded by Eurylochus, on the second, those under Parmenio".}

§§59-62

Then there is the case of Oreus.

Vocabulary

Nouns

δεσμωτήριον, τό	prison
ἅλωσις ἁλώσεως, ἡ	capture

Adjectives

ἄθλιος	wretched, miserable, abject
ἐπιτήδειος	suitable, fit; (with infin.) a fitting, deserving candidate for ...

Verbs

ἐπι-χαίρειν	derive malicious pleasure from someone's discomfiture, take a fiendish delight in ... ([dat.])
ἁλίσκεσθαι	(aor. infin. ἁλῶναι, partic. ἁλούς) be captured
τολμᾶν	dare, have the courage (to)
μαρτυρεῖν	bear witness, testify
ἀνθ-ίστασθαι	set oneself in opposition to, oppose

Adverb

τηνικαῦτα	at that (particular) time, at that juncture

60

Aids to comprehension

§59

Φιλιστίδης: An expedition (with troops supplied by Chalcis, Athens and Megara) would be sent to Oreus in the north of Euboea under the command of Cephisiphon, ending in summer 341 with the death of Philistides.

ἔπραττε: πράττειν with dative commonly bears the sense "act on someone's behalf", as his agent.

οἵ-περ: "the very men who".

ᾔδεσαν: Past tense of εἰδέναι, *MS* A.2.a.

Εὐφραῖος: A pupil of Plato, once sympathetic to the Macedonian cause, latterly its determined opponent.

ἐνθάδ': Here in Athens.

ὅπως ... ἔσονται: Supply ἔπραττε from above; cf. on §1.

§60

τὰ .. ἄλλ(α) ὡς ὑβρίζετο: Literally "as to how he was continually [imperfect] outraged in all other respects"; the speaker will pick out one sorry episode. We might translate "(... describe) all the various ways in which he was repeatedly subjected to outrages and insults".

προὐπηλακίζε(το): For the internal contraction cf. on προὔδοσαν in §56; προπηλακίζεσθαι = be treated to gross abuse, contumely.

εἴη: Neuter plural subject, hence singular verb: "there would be many things to tell", i.e. "it would require a long story/ take an age to describe ..."

πρότερον: Here with genitive, "[by] a year before".

ἐνέδειξεν: ἐν-δεικνύναι, "point out/ point the finger at", hence, in the context of formal legal proceedings, "file information against" by submitting an accusation to a magistrate with powers of arrest.

πράττουσιν: Present, harking back to the original perception.

συ-στραφέντες i.e. σύν + στρέφεσθαι, "club/ band together", aor. pass. participle.

χορηγόν: A χορηγός meets the cost of producing a chorus, hence here "paymaster": Philip runs the show.

πρυτανευόμενοι: "being controlled by a πρύτανις or ruler/ president/ chief magistrate", cuttingly for "under his supreme direction".

ἀπ-άγουσι: An instance of the so-called "historic" present, generally unacceptable in literary English, here an expression of the indignity to which Euphraeus was subjected: "they apprehend him [avail themselves of the procedure termed ἀπαγωγή, "summary arrest"] and carry him off to prison".

ὡς: "as", "on a charge of".

συν-ταράττοντα: (συν)ταράττειν means "throw into confusion, cause to be in turmoil", often with reference to political agitation: "for creating civil disorder" as a disturber of the peace.

§61

τοῦ ... βοηθεῖν ... ἀποτυμπανίσαι: Articular infinitives (*MS* B); ἀπο-τυμπανίζειν = "cudgel to death" — a punishment inflicted on common criminals.

ἐπ' with genitive, "in circumstances of", effectively "in possession of".

ὁπόσης: Like ὅσος (cf. on §21), "as much ... as".

ἔπραττον ὅπως with future (ληφθήσεται from λαμβάνειν): cf. on §1.

κατ-εσκευάζοντο τὴν πρᾶξιν: "proceeded to make arrangements for the execution <of their scheme>".

τῶν δὲ ... αἴσθοιτο: "while, among the democrats, if anybody (whoever) did perceive <what was going on>"; optative: *MS* D.2.b.

ἐσίγα καὶ κατ-επέπληκτο: "was silent and in a state of acute alarm/ consternation" (a pluperfect, see *MS* A.5 ~ perfect κατα-πέπληγμαι, from -πλήττεσθαι), "maintained a thoroughly dismayed silence".

οἵ: Cf. on §47.

μεμνημένοι: Perfect participle (*MS* A.4.a), plural in the wake of the generalising εἴ τις ..., "recalling as they did"; "Euphraeus, οἷα", i.e. "οἷα E.", or better, reflecting the prominence accorded to the name, "E. and οἷα".

ἀθλίως διέκειντο: Cf. on §4; "were in such a sorry state/ mess".

τοιούτου κακοῦ προσ-ιόντος: Genitive absolute (another at the start of §62); -ιόντος: see on παριόντες in §1.

ῥῆξαι φωνήν: "break [ῥηγνύναι] = break into speech", "break silence" or "speak out".

δια-σκευασάμενοι: "having fully prepared themselves" militarily.

προσ-ῄεσαν: Cf. on παριόντες in §1.

ἠμύνοντο ... προὐδίδοσαν: For the latter form see on §56; imperfects, "set about ..."

§62

(τῆς πόλεως) δ': Cf. on §5.

ἄρχουσι καὶ τυραννοῦσι: Not historic presents (cf. above), as they are commonly regarded: now that the city has been captured, it is ruled by tyrants.

ὁτιοῦν: "to treat E. in any way whatsoever [neuter of ὁστισοῦν, "anybody ..."]", "do absolutely anything to E.".

ἀπέσφαξεν: ἀπο-σφάττειν, "sever the throat of", then "kill", "do away with".

ἔργῳ μαρτυρήσας ... i.e. thus testifying on a practical level to both the honesty and the purity of his motives in ...

ἀνθ-ειστήκει: Pluperfect, *MS* A.5.

§§63-75

[63-66] Why did these people listen to Philip's advocates? It is because those who speak in the public interest cannot always gratify their audience, whereas their opponents do just that and thus advance the interests of Philip. The traitors had their way: this, I fear, may happen at Athens. Better die many times over than flatter Philip. Think of the fine recompense for their complaisance received by the men of Oreus, Eretria and Olynthus. [67-68] It is foolish to listen to the advocates of your enemies and to trust to the greatness of your city. No: you must have the foresight to do what must be done — unlike the men of Olynthus, of Oreus, of Phocis, and the rest of those who were ruined. [69] It is only as long as the ship is safe that every one should play his part in preventing its being overturned, but, once the waves have overwhelmed it, the effort is vain. [70] We then, so long as we are safe, we with our great city, what are we to do? I shall tell you, and I shall also move a resolution, and you shall vote for it it, if you are so disposed. We must take the lead in defending ourselves and providing ourselves with ships of war, and money, and troops. We at least must fight for freedom. [71] Next, we must send ambassadors in the hope of obtaining people to share the dangers and the expenditure, or of gaining time at least. [72] Such embassies were useful last year. [73-75] While protecting your own interests, you must send supplies to the troops in the Chersonese, besides summoning and advising the other Greeks, in keeping with the high prestige enjoyed by your city. You cannot leave it to the men of Chalcis and Megara to save Greece, while you run away from your obligations. That duty has been bequeathed to you by your ancestors as a privilege won at the cost of many great dangers. There is nothing to be gained, and everything to lose, by sitting idle.

Vocabulary
Nouns

ἄγνοια, ἡ	ignorance
κακία, ἡ	cowardice
ἀφορμή, ἡ	starting-point (for a project), plur. resources, advantages
σπουδή, ἡ	zeal, exertion, determined effort
κυβερνήτης, ὁ	pilot
κοινωνός, ὁ	sharer, partner (in, gen.)
ὄφελος, τό	use, benefit, good
σκάφος, τό	vessel, ship
ἰσχύς, ἡ	strength, power
γέρας, τό	prerogative, privilege
ἀνάλωμα -ατος, τό	expense, expenditure

Adjectives

ἀλλότριος	belonging to someone else
μάταιος	(-ος -ον, also -ος -α -ον) vain, idle, pointless
πρόθυμος	zealous, exerting oneself to the utmost
σῶος	safe

Verbs

ἀπ-ελαύνειν	(aor. -έλασαι) drive away, expel
ἐπι-τρέπειν	entrust
κατα-λείπειν	leave behind, bequeath
συμ-πράττειν	(with dat.) act/ cooperate with
φάσκειν	assert, allege
κήδεσθαι	(with gen.) be concerned about
φείδεσθαι	(with gen.) spare, be merciful to
ὁρμᾶν	set out (from a base, to launch an attack on)
προ-ορᾶσθαι	(middle) foresee
νουθετεῖν	advise, admonish
συγ-χωρεῖν	(with infin.) consent (to)
ὠθεῖν	(imperf. ἐώθουν) push/ thrust aside
ἐν-διδόναι	give up, surrender

Adverb

ἐνίοτε	sometimes, at times

Asseverative particle

νή	(with acc.) (yes) by ...

Aids to comprehension
§63

τί .. ποτ' αἴτιον: "what can the reason be", cf. on §43.

θαυμάζετ' ἴσως: Parenthetic.

τὸ ... ἔχειν: Articular infinitive, with accusatives serving as subjects (*MS* B); accusative τό here rather than a straightforward τοῦ (the "vulgate" reading), "the reason for the fact that the Olynthians ... were": "with regard to-the Olynthians-to", i.e. "for their ... -ing".

ἥδιον ... ἔχειν: ἡδέως ἔχειν πρός τινα means "be pleasant/ agreeable/ favourably disposed towards one".

ὅπερ ...: Supply αἴτιόν ἐστιν, "the very (-περ) one that applies among you [here in Athens]/ in your case [too: English can dispense with this element]".

οὐδὲ βουλομένοις i.e. there are times when it is not actually possible for them, even when/ though they wish to, to ...

πρὸς χάριν: "to gratify/ entertain you" (and win popularity for themselves).

τὰ γάρ ...: Neuter plural subject, singular verb (cf. γένοιτο in §65); τὰ .. πράγματα (heading the sentence): "it is the state/ your political system that ..."

σκοπεῖν ὅπως with future: cf. on §1.

ἐν αὐτοῖς οἷς χαρίζονται: "in (putting forward) the very arguments whereby they court popularity", by seeking to gratify their listeners (cf. πρὸς χάριν above).

§64

εἰσφέρειν ἐκέλευον: Subject the patriots, as with <ἐκέλευον> πολεμεῖν ... below
~ οἱ δ᾽ their opponents: "they called for a war-tax". εἰσ-φέρειν, "bring in", in the sense of levying an εἰσ-φορά, an extraordinary tax on property to raise funds for conducting a war.

ἐγ-κατ-ελήφθησαν (~ -λαμβάνειν): "they were caught in <the situation they had created for themselves>", "were trapped".

τἆλλα [τὰ ἄλλα] ... πάνθ᾽: "<they proposed> everything else in the same fashion [cf. on §33]", i.e. "and so with everything else they advocated".

οἶμαι = οἴομαι, a dismissive parenthesis.

ἵνα μὴ ...: Final clause, *MS* C.4.a; "in order not to speak of each and every one at a time", i.e. "and so [see above] — I need not dwell on the details of each particular case — with ..."

ἐφ᾽ οἷς χαριοῦνται: "(arguments) on the basis/ strength of which they would win favour" by telling their listeners what they wanted to hear.

ἐξ ὧν ...: Supply ταῦτ᾽ ἔλεγον from the preceding clause: "(arguments) as a result of which they were going to be saved", that is "which would ensure their safety".

πολλὰ ... προσίεντο: "many things and <I mean by this> the last things, the majority/ the people did not admit [προσ-ίεσθαι]", i.e. "many of their proposals — those in the final stages <of the proceedings> — they did not come to accept ..."

οὐχ οὕτως ... πρὸς χάριν: "not ... just [οὕτως "just like that", "simply"] out of a desire for gratification".

ὑπο-κατα-κλινόμενοι: "through lying down [submissively, throwing in the towel] beneath <the weight of those working on them>", "yielding to the pressure".

τοῖς ὅλοις ἡττᾶσθαι: τὰ ὅλα, "one's all, the sum total of one's interests"; dative = "(be worsted) in respect of the whole situation", i.e. "that they were being comprehensively beaten", "fighting a completely lost cause".

ἐνόμιζον: Imperfect = "they began to believe".

§65

ὅ: Relative serving as sentence-connective.

δέδοικ(α)/ εἰδῆτ(ε): Perfects: *MS* A.3.a/2.a.

μή/ ἐπειδάν with subjunctive: *MS* C.4.b/3.a.

εἰδῆτ' with participle, "come to know, realise that ... "

ἐκ-λογιζόμενοι: "by reflecting on the issue".

μὴ γένοιτο: Optative to express a wish: *MS* D.4; "may not events turn out to be in this position": "I hope and pray that things do not come to this!"

τεθνάναι: On the form see *MS* A.3.a; "to die", the perfect stressing the finality of the process.

μυριάκις: "ten thousand/ countless times", as we might say "a thousand times over".

{καὶ ... τινάς: "or to sacrifice any of those who speak for your good."}

καλήν γ': Sarcastically, "a fine ... indeed!"

ἀπ-ειλήφασιν: Perfect of ἀπο-λαμβάνειν (*MS* A.3.b), with χάριν "receive (due) reward/ recompense".

§66

πρέσβεις: Sent at the instigation of Demosthenes in 343/2 before the tyrannies were established.

Κλειτάρχῳ: Cf. on §58.

δουλεύουσί γε ...: γε exclamatory, as in καλήν γ' above: "yes, they are slaves indeed — whipped and butchered!"

καλῶς .. ἐφείσατο: "fine mercy he showed to ..."

Λασθένην: Usually coupled with one Euthycrates as betrayer of Olynthus to Philip; cf. in §56.

ἵππαρχον: "cavalry-commander".

§67

καὶ κακῶς ...: Accusative and infinitive construction, in the wake of the implied subject of the preceding infinitive (a general "that people should ...").

ὧν = τούτων ἅ.

τηλικαύτην = τοσαύτην, reinforced by accusative τὸ μέγεθος ("in respect of ..."): "of such greatness and eminence".

ὥστε ... πείσεσθαι: "that one would suffer no serious harm, not even if anything whatsoever proves to be the case", i.e. "no matter what may happen", "come what may". πείσεσθαι is future infinitive of πάσχειν; for μηδ' ἄν see *MS* C.2; and for ὁτιοῦν the note on §62.

§68

καὶ μὴν ...: "and what is more, that thing [ἐκεῖνο contemptuous] certainly is disgraceful", i. e. "in addition, what is really discreditable is to come out at some [ποτ'] later date with".

γάρ: In an incredulous question, "why", "really".

ἂν ᾠήθη: Aorist of οἴεσθαι. Verbs of thinking/ saying etc. are found from time to time with aorist infinitive to refer to future time (ἄν is sometimes imported in such cases by modern editors; it may be that here as elsewhere the force of ἄν was felt to extend to the infinitive also): "who would have thought that this would happen?"

... ἔδει γάρ: "yes by Zeus, because" ~ "heavens yes, <it's happened> because ..."

τὸ καὶ τό: "this thing and that thing" = "this or that", followed up with a single τό, "this".

τότ': Pulled forward for emphasis.

ἀπ-ολωλότων: Perfect (*MS* A.3.a), sense "have perished/ been destroyed, be done for".

§69

ἕως ἄν with present subjunctive, "as long as": *MS* C.3.b.

ἄν τε .. ἄν τ' with subjunctive, "whether ... or": *MS* C.2.

μεῖζον ... ἔλαττον: Polar opposites, hence "contrasting" comparatives (cf. on μείζονος in §16), which we put in positive form: "big/ small".

πάντ' ἄνδρ' ἑξῆς: "every man in his turn".

ὅπως (with future) ... σκοπεῖσθαι: "watch to ensure that ...", cf. on §1.

ἑκὼν .. ἄκων: "deliberately .. accidentally".

ἀνα-τρέψει: "overturn, cause to capsize".

ἐπειδάν with aorist subjunctive: *MS* C.3.a.

ὑπέρ-σχῃ: Aorist subjunctive of ὑπερ-έχειν, intransitively, "extend over/ above a point": "has flooded over her".

§70

ἀξίωμα: Here (ctr. note on §43) the "esteem, prestige" enjoyed by a city of the very first rank.

ποιῶμεν: Deliberative subjunctive, *MS* C.5(i).

πάλαι ... κάθηται: The main emphasis falls on the participle (literally "perhaps someone long sits [πάλαι with present, where we would say "has been sitting"] who would with pleasure have asked"): "maybe someone sitting <here now> has long been wanting to put this question". ἐρωτήσας is a modern correction: the MSS have an intractable future participle.

ἐρῶ serves as future of λέγω.

καὶ γράψω δέ: "and what is more [καί] I shall put forward a motion [cf. on §8]".

ἄν = ἐάν, with subjunctive: *MS* C.2.

τριήρεσι ... λέγω: "with warships ... I mean".

καὶ γὰρ ἄν: "because even if": *MS* C.2.

δήπου: "let us presume", taking the worst case.

ἡμῖν γ᾽: Dative of agent (cf. on §45) with the verbal adjective ἀγωνιστέον (~ ἀγωνίζεσθαι): "*we* at least must contend/ engage in the struggle".

§71

ταῦτα δὴ ... φανερά picks up the two present participles after the interruption τριήρεσι ... ἀγωνιστέον: "once we .. have completed all these preparations [middle-passive perfect participle, *MS* A.4.b] then, and when we have made them clear (let them be seen to have been made)".

ἤδη: "then (and only then)".

παρα-καλῶμεν/ ἐκ-πέμπωμεν: First person commands, "let us ...", "we can ...": *MS* C.5(ii).

τοὺς .. διδάξοντας: Future participle expressing purpose, "men on (official) embassies to put them in the picture about these developments".

{πανταχοῖ ... καταστρέψασθαι: "in all directions — to the Peloponnese, to Rhodes, to Chios, to the king; for it is not unimportant for his interests either that Philip should be prevented from subjugating the world."}

ἵν᾽ ...: Final clause, *MS* C.4.a.

ἐάν with subjunctive: *MS* C.2.

ἄν τι δέῃ (subjunctive of δεῖ): ibid.

εἰ δὲ μή: "or if not"; εἰ δὲ μή is the usual way of saying "otherwise", even when an ἐάν clause has preceded.

χρόνους ... πράγμασιν: "you may at least create/ insert periods of time in the proceedings", i.e. "... delay the march of events".

§72

ἄνδρα i.e. a single man (to whom something could happen at any time).

συν-εστώσης: Intransitive perfect participle (*MS* A.3.b) of συν-ιστάναι, "consolidated", "tightly knit", not liable to fall apart.

οὐδὲ ... οὐδ᾽: "not even ... <is> ..., any more than <were> ..."

τοῦτ᾽: Delaying tactics.

ἄχρηστον: Cf. in §40.

πέρυσιν: An adverb, "last year".

καὶ κατηγορίαι: "embassies and denunciations" amounts to "embassies, embassies of denunciation".

ἃς ... περιήλθομεν: "(embassies) on which we went around/went in the course of our tour" of the Peloponnese.

ἐκεινοσί: ἐκεῖνος indicates that he is well-known to the audience, -ί that he is present at this moment (cf. on §§3, 12).

καὶ ἐποιήσαμεν ...: Greek often switches from a relative to a main clause where we would tend to hold on to the former: "and <in which>".

ἐποιήσαμεν: With infinitive, "cause to".

ἐπι-σχεῖν: Aorist infinitive of ἐπ-έχειν, used intransitively in the sense "pause, stop, desist".

§73

λέγω ...: "say/ recommend that you should ..."

μηδὲν ... ἐθέλοντας: The participle has conditional force.

αὐτοὺς ὑπὲρ αὑτῶν: Cf. on §2.

καὶ γάρ: "because in point of fact".

εὔηθες here with accusative and infinitive, "it is foolish/ idiotic that you should", "for you to".

τὰ οἰκεῖ' .. προϊεμένους: For the verb see on §1: "while sacrificing your own interests".

τῶν μελλόντων: Cf. on §2.

τοῖς .. ἐν Χερρονήσῳ: Diopeithes and his mercenaries.

ἀποστέλλειν: Cf. in §15.

τἄλλ': τὰ ἄλλα.

ὅσ(α): Cf. on §21.

συγκαλεῖν ...: An unlinked run of infinitives designed to press home the point that Athens must take the initiative: "to convoke, to convene, to instruct, to admonish".

ἐστὶ (neuter plural subject) πόλεως: "is the duty of ...", cf. on §12.

ἀξίωμ(α): Cf. on §70.

ἡλίκον = ὅσον, literally "(a reputation) as great as is available [cf. on §5] to you", i.e. "as great as that enjoyed by your own (city)".

§74

Χαλκιδέας ... Μεγαρέας: In the course of 342 Athens had found an (eventual) ally in Callias of Chalcis in Euboea, and in early 341 a formal alliance was concluded. For Megara, cf. on §17.

ἀπο-δράσεσθαι: Future of ἀπο-διδράσκειν, a verb often applied to runaway slaves, deserters and the like, and so a cutting word for the evasion of one's duties: "run away from the tasks confronting you/ your responsibilities" (πράγματα = "things of importance", "what matters to/ concerns one").

ἀγαπητόν: "<it is a matter> with which one has to be content", i.e. one may be thankful [as they certainly will be] if each one of these states [ἕκαστοι] manages to secure its own survival. ἐάν with subjunctive: MS C.2.

ἀλλ' ὑμῖν τοῦτο πρακτέον: "no, it is by you that this <job of saving Greece> has to be carried out/ seen through"; verbal adjective (~ πράττειν), with dative to express personal agent (cf. on §45).

ὑμῖν οἱ πρόγονοι ...: Emphatic asyndeton: "it was for you that ..."

μετά i.e. <a γέρας won> by undergoing ...

§75

καθεδεῖται: Future of καθέζεσθαι, "sit", often "sit doing nothing"; future with εἰ, "is going to, means to", cf. on §10.

ὅπως ... σκοπῶν: "looking for a way to avoid taking any action personally", cf. on §1.

οὐδὲ μήποθ' εὕρῃ: οὐ μή with subjunctive (usually aorist) to express an emphatic denial (*MS* C.5(iii)): "he will most certainly never actually track down", "there is definitely no prospect of his actually finding".

τοὺς ποιήσοντας: "those who will act" = "anybody who will/ to act".

ἔπειτ': Cf. on §9.

δέδοιχ': Perfect: *MS* A.3.a; here with ὅπως μή + future indicative, "that ... will" rather than "may".

ὅσ(α): Cf. on §21.

§76

These then are my proposals. Adopt these proposals, and it is my belief that our position may even yet be retrieved. If any one can offer better advice, let him speak; and may what you are about to determine be in your best interests.

Aids to comprehension
§76

μὲν δή: Resumptively, "well then".

ταῦτα twice: note the position of these pronouns.

γράφω: Cf. on §8.

ἐπανορθωθῆναι: Cf. on §4.

τούτων γιγνομένων: Genitive absolute with conditional force.

λεγέτω καὶ συμβουλευέτω: Third singular imperatives, "let him ..."

δόξει: Note the future tense: whatever you are about to decide, not (purely indefinitely) may decide.

συν-ενέγκοι: Aorist optative of συμ-φέρειν, expressing a wish: *MS* D.4.

SUGGESTIONS FOR FURTHER READING

For an excellent short introduction to Demosthenes and other representatives of the genre see M. Edwards, *The Attic Orators* (Bristol, 1994); his first chapter deals succinctly with early oratory, oratory and rhetoric in the fifth and fourth centuries, deliberative, forensic and epideictic oratory, and the canon of ten Attic orators, while general studies of Demosthenes are listed on p.85. Cf. also on features of style and historical background G.A. Kennedy in *The Cambridge History of Classical Literature* I, edd. P.E. Easterling and B.M.W. Knox (Cambridge, 1985), 514-23, 800-02, and the introductions in A.N.W. Saunders, *Greek Political Oratory* (Harmondsworth, 1970; transl. of *Philippic* iii: pp. 249-63), E.I. McQueen, *Demosthenes: Olynthiacs* (Bristol, 1986), S. Usher, *Demosthenes: De Corona* (Warminster, 1993).

Notable among annotated editions of *Philippic* iii in English is that of J.E. Sandys (London, rev. edn, 1933). Short analyses: L. Pearson, *The Art of Demosthenes* (*Beiträge zur klassischen Philologie* 68, Meisenham am Glan, 1976), 36-8, 152-5; style: C.W. Wooten, 'A Few Observations on Form and Content in Demosthenes', *Phoenix* 31 (1977), 258-61.

For various approaches to the problems posed by the longer and shorter versions (so-called) see D.F. Jackson and G.O. Rowe, 'Demosthenes 1915-1965', *Lustrum* 14 (1969), 70-1; also R. Sealey in *Revue des études grecques* 68 (1955), 101ff.; L. Pearson op.cit. above, 150ff.; W. Bühler, 'Tendenzen nachdemosthenischen Bearbeitung der 3. Philippischen Rede des Demosthenes', *Kuklos: Rudolf Keydell zum neunzigsten Geburtstag* (Berlin and New York, 1978), 59-77; early evidence: see the remarks of J.E.G. Whitehorne in *Oxyrhynchus Papyri*, vol. lxiii (1995), p.118.

On Philip II specifically see the brief account in S. Hornblower, *The Greek World 479-323 BC* (London and New York, rev. edn, 1991), 239-60; bibliography p. 326. Lists, with dates, of Philip's activities: J.R. Ellis, *Philip II and Macedonian Imperialism* (London, 1976), 14-20; N.G.L. Hammond and G.T. Griffith, *A History of Macedonia* II (Oxford, 1979), 722-6. See also N.G.L. Hammond, *Philip of Macedon* (London, 1994).